TESS OF THE
D'URBERVILLES

Unorthodox Beauty

D1563013

TWAYNE'S MASTERWORK STUDIES

Robert Lecker, General Editor

TESS OF THE D'URBERVILLES

Unorthodox Beauty

PETER J. CASAGRANDE

Twayne Publishers • New York
Maxwell Macmillan Canada • Toronto
Maxwell Macmillan International • New York   Oxford   Singapore   Sydney

Twayne's Masterwork Studies No. 87

Tess of the d'Urbervilles: Unorthodox Beauty
Peter J. Casagrande

Twayne Publishers
Macmillan Publishing Company
866 Third Avenue
New York, New York 10022

Maxwell Macmillan Canada, Inc.
1200 Eglinton Avenue East
Suite 200
Don Mills, Ontario M3C 3N1

Macmillan Publishing Company is part of the Maxwell Communication Group of Companies.

Library of Congress Cataloging-in-Publication Data
Casagrande, Peter J.
    Tess of the d'Urbervilles : unorthodox beauty / Peter J. Casagrande.
       p.   cm.—(Twayne's masterwork studies ; no. 87)
    Includes bibliographical references and index.
    ISBN 0-8057-9418-2 (alk. paper)—ISBN 0-8057-8558-2 (pbk. : alk. paper)
    1. Hardy, Thomas, 1840–1928.   Tess of the d'Urbervilles.
I. Title. II. Series.
PR4748.C33   1992
823'.8—dc20   91-34019
                                          CIP

10 9 8 7 6 5 4 3 2 1 (hc)
10 9 8 7 6 5 4 3 2   (pb)

Printed in the United States of America

For
Alvera Giovanna Casagrande
(1907–1990)

Never in English prose literature was such a seer of beauty as Thomas Hardy.
—Arnold Bennett

The business of the poet and novelist is to show the sorriness underlying the grandest things, and the grandeur underlying the sorriest things.
—Thomas Hardy

CONTENTS

Thomas Hardy, 1891
Photograph by Barraud

Note on the References
and Acknowledgments

All references to *Tess* are to the World's Classics paperback edition, edited by Juliet Grindle and Simon Gatrell (New York: Oxford University Press, 1988). Excerpts from "The Ruined Maid" and "In Tenebris II" are taken from *The Complete Poems of Thomas Hardy,* ed. James Gibson (New York: Macmillan Publishing Company, 1978).

I am most deeply grateful to my wife, Pamela, for her love and for her refusal to be discouraged throughout some difficult times. I am indebted to Cynthia Bachofer, Thomas David, Michael Guemple, Dawn Hayward, Sung Ryol Kim, and Jennifer Thompson, graduate scholars and teachers at the University of Kansas, for sharing with me their opinions about *Tess* in a seminar on the novel in the fall of 1989. I wish I had space to name and thank the many, many undergraduates at Kansas with whom I have read and discussed *Tess,* as well as Hardy's other novels, over the years. Their questions have taught me a great deal about Hardy's novels, and I am fortunate to be able to refer to certain of their opinions throughout my study. To Elizabeth Casagrande, student of philosophy at the University of Kansas, I tender very special thanks for assisting me with the research for this book; for reading portions of the typescript at several stages of its development; and for speaking so instructively with me about "unorthodox beauty" and other things that entered into the writing. She will recognize, and I hope enjoy, her many contributions throughout. Financial support from the University of Kansas General Research Fund freed me from other duties and enabled me to complete much of the work for this study in 1988–89.

Note on the References and Acknowledgments

On 12 April 1990, my mother, Alvera G. Casagrande, died suddenly after a long life devoted, to its very end, to the instruction of her husband and her three sons. I take this opportunity to remember, as if one could forget, the love, the unwavering confidence, interest, and support.

CHRONOLOGY:
THOMAS HARDY'S LIFE AND WORKS

1840   Thomas Hardy III born 2 June, the eldest of four children of Thomas and Jemima Hardy, in a village in the rural county of Dorset, in the English West Country. Hardy's father is a builder with several men in his employ; his mother is unusually well-read for a woman of her station.

1848   Enters Stinsford National School, a village school sponsored by the wife of a local landowner.

1849–1855   Attends the Dorchester British School several miles from his home, where he studies Latin, French, and mathematics and proves to be a superior student.

1856   Leaves school to be apprenticed to a Dorchester architect and church restorer (until 1860). Witnesses the hanging of a woman for the murder of her husband, an experience that may have contributed to the story of Tess and particularly the closing scene of *Tess of the d'Urbervilles*.

1856–1860   Continues to study Latin and begins studying Greek; meets the Dorset poet William Barnes and becomes friends with author and reviewer Horace M. Moule, son of a prominent Dorchester clergyman.

1860   Goes to work as an architectural assistant. Moule introduces him to a number of controversial theological and scientific writings (including Charles Darwin's *On the Origin of Species*). Hardy begins writing poetry.

1862   Moves to London to work as an architectural draftsman; elected to the Architectural Association.

1863   Wins a prize from the Royal Institute of British Architects for the essay "On the Application of Coloured Bricks and Terra Cotta to Modern Architecture." Looking to possible work as a writer of book reviews and art criticism, begins reading

Chronology

	widely in English writers (the Elizabethans, Shelley, Keats, Scott, Browning, Tennyson, Spencer, Huxley, and Mill).

1865   His story "How I Built Myself a House" appears in a prominent journal. Unsuccessfully attempts to publish some of his poems. Investigates entering Cambridge University to prepare for a career in the Church but sets aside his plan because of religious doubt.

1867   Returns to his native Dorset to resume work there as an architectural assistant and church restorer (until 1869); begins writing a novel, "The Poor Man and the Lady" (never published); falls in love with Tryphena Sparks and may have become engaged to her.

1870   Begins a second novel, *Desperate Remedies* (1871); travels to St. Juliot, Cornwall, to oversee restoration of a church; in Cornwall he meets Emma Lavinia Gifford, sister-in-law of the incumbent.

1871   *Desperate Remedies,* his first published novel, appears. Returning to Weymouth to help his old employer with church restorations, he begins work on a third novel, *Under the Greenwood Tree* (1872) and makes notes for a fourth, *A Pair of Blue Eyes* (1873).

1872   Possibly breaks his engagement with Tryphena Sparks to become engaged to Emma Gifford; gives up architecture for novel writing; Leslie Stephen, a leading editor and critic, requests a serial narrative from Hardy (*Far from the Madding Crowd* [1874]); his friend Horace Moule commits suicide at Cambridge.

1874   *Far from the Madding Crowd* receives more praise from reviewers than any novel Hardy has published thus far; Hardy and Emma marry.

1875–1878   The couple takes up residence in London; Hardy begins work (1875–76) on *The Hand of Ethelberta* (1876), and the next year on *The Return of The Native* (1878); the latter novel is the first of his great tragic novels.

1878–1880   Begins writing *The Trumpet-Major* (1880) and publishes "The Distracted Young Preacher," the first of many short stories he will publish; begins work on *A Laodicean* (1881).

1882   Returns with Emma to live in Dorset, where he begins writing *Two on a Tower* (1882).

1883   The native returns to Dorset for the final time to build a fashionable house (Max Gate) near Dorchester and not far from his parents' cottage.

Chronology

1884	Begins writing *The Mayor of Casterbridge* (1886), the second of his tragic masterpieces; his growing reputation wins him social invitations from distinguished people.
1885	The Hardys move into Max Gate.
1886	Begins writing *The Woodlanders* (1887).
1887	Tillotson & Son Publishers offers him the generous sum of one thousand guineas for the future *Tess of the d'Urbervilles* (1891)—more money than he had ever been offered for a story.
1888	Publishes his first collection of short stories, *Wessex Tales*; also publishes "The Profitable Reading of Fiction," the first of three important essays on the writing and reading of fiction (the other two are "Candour in English Fiction" [1889] and "The Science of Fiction" [1891]); planning *Tess*, he visits the farm he will use in the pivotal wedding night episode (chapters 34–36).
1889	Tillotson rejects approximately the first half of the narrative that will become *Tess* on grounds of bad taste; Hardy can find no publisher to consider it unless he removes the offending passages.
1891	Serializes an amended version of *Tess* in the *Graphic* and later in this year publishes it in three volumes, with most of the offending passages restored; publishes a second volume of short stories, *A Group of Noble Dames*.
1892	Publishes *The Pursuit of the Well-Beloved*; begins work on *Jude the Obscure* (1895).
1894	Publishes *Life's Little Ironies*, his third volume of short stories; hostile reviews of *Jude* possibly contribute to his decision to give up writing novels to write poetry.
1896	Writes a group of important poems, among them the "In Tenebris" trilogy and "Wessex Heights."
1897	Publishes *The Well-Beloved*, an extensive revision of the 1892 serial.
1898	Publishes *Wessex Poems*, his first book of verse, consisting mainly of poems written in the 1860s and 1890s.
1901	Hardy publishes *Poems of the Past and the Present*.
1903–1909	Publishes *The Dynasts*, an epic poem based on the Napoleonic Wars, and a third volume of poems, *Time's Laughingstocks* (1909).
1910	With the deaths of George Meredith and Charles Swinburne (in 1908), Hardy stands as the greatest living English writer and receives the Order of Merit in 1910.

Chronology

1912	Hardy publishes the Wessex edition of his novels and poems; receives the gold medal of the Royal Society of Literature; his wife Emma dies suddenly in November.
1913	Magdalene College (Cambridge) makes Hardy an honorary fellow; Hardy publishes *A Changed Man,* his fourth and final volume of short stories.
1914	Hardy marries Florence Dugdale; publishes a volume of poems, *Satires of Circumstance.*
1917	Publishes his fifth volume of poems, *Moments of Vision*; begins writing, with Florence's aid, the autobiography to be published (as if it were a biography by Florence) as *The Early Life of Thomas Hardy* (1928) and *The Later Years of Thomas Hardy* (1930).
1920	Hardy receives the honorary degree of Doctor of Letters at Oxford University.
1922	Hardy publishes *Late Lyrics and Earlier* with an important preface.
1924	Hardy adapts *Tess* to the stage and sees the play performed in Dorchester and London.
1925	Hardy publishes *Human Shows Far Phantasies Songs and Trifles,* his seventh volume of poems and the last to be published while he is living.
1928	Hardy dies on 11 January; his final book of poems, *Winter Words,* appears after his death.

Literary and Historical Context

1

Reforming the Reformers

Thomas Hardy was born into the early Victorian world when widespread parliamentary reforms were under way—changes driven by an aggressively optimistic belief that the conditions of human life could be improved through rational effort. Because he was a man of humble beginnings and first-rate talent, this quality of his era was naturally of great interest and appeal to him. Eight years before Hardy's birth in a tiny village some 150 miles west of London, the passage in Parliament of the great Reform Bill of 1832 altered significantly the balance of political power established some 150 years before, in 1688, because parliamentary representation was granted to segments of the commercial and industrial classes that had never before been enfranchised.

In 1867, when Hardy was in London and was just beginning his career as a writer of fiction, the second reform bill reduced the property qualifications for parliamentary voters, thus extending voting rights to an even greater number of male citizens. In 1884, just a few years before he began writing *Tess of the d'Urbervilles*, a third reform bill extended to male laborers in the counties the vote already given workingmen in the boroughs. It comes as little surprise, then, that when Hardy submitted his first novel to Macmillan—the never published "Poor Man and the Lady," which he wrote in the late 1860s—the publisher considered the manuscript too politically volatile for publication, apparently because Hardy's writing was too strongly inclined toward the working class. Although Hardy was of the lower-middle class, during his early years in rural Dorset he had lived in close contact with working-class families. As a boy, he had known the son of a laborer who was paid only a few shillings a week and cottage rent. That boy had starved to death, and an autopsy showed he had nothing but raw turnips in his stomach.

Nor was Hardy's experience of human misery limited to that of the rural poor. Five years in London (1862–67) exposed him to the urban poverty that Charles Dickens portrays in novels such as *Oliver Twist* and *Bleak House*. Hardy was critical of much of what he observed in society. Throughout his fiction he uses the lower-class observer as a device for noting the defects of persons of superior social station. Although Hardy himself never suffered poverty or hunger, as a member of an underclass, and as the son of a woman who had worked as a domestic servant, he could be angrily sensitive to the deprivations of others, most particularly those who, like Tess Durbeyfield, were unlikely to benefit measurably from social or political reform. Hardy is not a political novelist in the ordinary sense, but throughout his writings he displays an awareness of the views of leading political, social, and intellectual reformers—such as John Stuart Mill, Thomas Henry Huxley, Charles Darwin, and others—as well as the views of radically reformist poets such as Percy Shelley and Charles Swinburne.

Yet if Hardy sympathized with the widespread desire to improve the human lot, in a fundamental way he doubted that it was possible to do so. That is, while he shared the reformers' aims, he could not stomach their optimism, what he considered their unexamined belief that the condition of men and women could be improved. In fact, Hardy used reformist optimism as a prevailing philosophy against which to form a philosophy and art of his own. It is correct, with proper reservations, to describe Hardy's art as an attempt to display the beauty in the defect he unveiled with his relentless pessimism.

Reforming the Reformers

"If way to the Better there be," Hardy wrote in the poem "In Tenebris II" (1895–96), "it exacts a full look at the Worst." This poem of self-anguish is worth noting briefly here because it exposes Hardy's fundamental creative stance, his simultaneously deep engagement with and estrangement from the fervent belief in progress of his age:

> When the clouds' swoln bosoms echo back the shouts of the many
>   and strong
> That things are all as they best may be, save a few to be right ere long,
> And my eyes have not the vision in them to discern what to these is
>   so clear,
> The blot seems straightway in me alone; one better he were not here.
>
> The stout upstanders say, All's well with us: ruers have nought to rue!
> And what the potent say so oft, can it fail to be somewhat true?
> Breezily go they, breezily come; their dust smokes around their career,
> Till I think I am one born out of due time, who has no calling here.
>
> Their dawns bring lusty joys, it seems; their evenings all that is sweet;
> Our times are blessed times, they cry: Life shapes it as is most meet,
> And nothing is much the matter; there are many smiles to a tear;
> Then what is the matter is I, I say. Why should such an one be
>   here? . . .
>
> Let him in whose ears the low-voiced Best is killed by the clash of the
>   First,
> Who holds that if way to the Better there be, it exacts a full look at
>   the Worst,
> Who feels that delight is a delicate growth cramped by crookedness,
>   custom, and fear,
> Get him up and be gone as one shaped awry; he disturbs the order here.[1]

In his suggestion that "the Worst" is something repellent as well as strangely appealing lies one reason for Hardy's continuing importance. His is a passionately private vision feeding rebelliously off a powerful public one expressed by poets of the stature of William Wordsworth, Alfred Lord Tennyson, and Robert Browning. Hardy's epigraph for "In Tenebris II," from Psalm 142, is a cry of isolation and a cry of defiance: "I looked on my right hand, and beheld; but there was no man that would know me. . . . no man cared for my soul" (*Complete Poems*, 168). Hardy continues to appeal because he directs his pessimism not at the flaws he finds in humanity but at something much more formidable, the defects he sees in the very nature of things. Because he believed that humanity had evolved to a level of feeling and understanding that the conditions of human existence would constantly frustrate, his art constitutes a grand counterstatement to the prevailing optimism of the Victorian age, as well as to the surviving optimisms of our own age.

In Hardy's unprecedented ways of diverging from the noisy optimists of his times lie the originalities of his art. He chose not to go with the flow, so to speak, and so we find him opposing the war in South Africa in the late 1890s, as well as the war in Europe from 1914 to 1917. When during the First World War he lost a favorite nephew who was the son and heir his marriages never produced, Hardy said that any conception he may have retained of a fundamental ultimate wisdom at the root of things was given the death blow. And out of this same unease with what he termed in *The Dynasts* (1903–1908) "the intolerable antilogy of making figments feel,"[2] we find him fashioning throughout his novels a series of unforgettable heroines struggling to escape the always confining, at times crushing, roles imposed on them by patriarchal institutions. Hardy probes the roots of war and social oppression not just in the natures of men and women and in the structures of society but also in that defective Nature of which flawed human nature was for him but a part. We find him sharply critical, throughout his career, of what he regarded as the miserable failure of institutional Christianity to either explain or improve the unhappy lot of men and women.

Hardy's success in attempting to re-form the reformist views of his age through novels and poetry is most evident in his public's frequently baffled, sometimes outraged, but almost always admiring response to his genius and his dangerous iconoclasm. From the reader for Macmillan who in 1869 warned him that "The Poor Man and the Lady" could not be published because of its radical politics, to the reviewer for the *Quarterly Review* who in 1892 found *Tess* a "clumsy sordid tale of boorish brutality and lust," to the Bishop of Wakefield who in 1896 wrote a letter to the papers announcing that he had tossed *Jude the Obscure* into the fire,[3] the Victorian public knew not what to make of a writer at once so deeply, eloquently humane and so subversively, aggressively reformist.

2

The Importance of the Work

Tess of the d'Urbervilles is the product of Hardy's fascination with women of beauty, energy, and intelligence who find themselves trapped between these gifts, the aspirations such gifts justify, and their society's assumption that respectable women must be either submissive or unobtrusively and harmlessly aspiring. With few exceptions, Hardy's most interesting characters are his unconventional women— Fancy Day of *Under the Greenwood Tree* (1871), Bathsheba Everdene of *Far from the Madding Crowd* (1874), Ethelberta Petherwin of the too seldom read *Hand of Ethelberta* (1876), Eustacia Vye of *The Return of the Native* (1878), Marty South of *The Woodlanders* (1887), Sue Bridehead and Arabella Donn of *Jude the Obscure* (1895), and Tess Durbeyfield, who, with sisters so unconventional both before and after, is, predictably, both the conventional ruined maid of fiction and a ruined maid like no other that has ever existed in British fiction.

Hardy's originality in *Tess* is best evaluated by noting the ways in which his Tess differs from that long line of sexually victimized women of British fiction that begins most conspicuously with Samuel Richardson's *Clarissa* (1747–48) and continues into the nineteenth century in important novels such as Sir Walter Scott's *Heart of Midlothian*

The Importance of the Work

(1818), Charles Dickens's *David Copperfield* (1849–50), Elizabeth Gaskell's *Ruth* (1857), and George Eliot's *Adam Bede* (1859) and *Mill on the Floss* (1860). These classic portraits of sexual ruin coexisted with equally popular dramatizations on the Victorian stage and depictions in Victorian painting of the fallen woman. The central figure is usually pitiful, shame-filled, mute, groveling, doomed, and always, because she is the mythic daughter of Eve, in some way blameworthy.[4]

In Hardy's first major novel, *Far from the Madding Crowd,* this conventional figure is the pathetic Fanny Robin, a servant girl seduced by a deceiving sergeant of the cavalry, and she plays opposite a resourceful, sexually aggressive heroine, Bathsheba Everdene. Fanny narrowly misses the chance to gain respectability through marriage when she mistakenly goes to one church for the ceremony while Sergeant Troy waits at another. Ultimately she dies a miserable death in childbirth at a workhouse. Hardy's unease with this conventional figure of ruin is clear because he also includes Bathsheba in this novel— an extraordinary character who is more than the intellectual and emotional equal of the three men who court her.

By the time he wrote *Far from the Madding Crowd* Hardy had already broken decisively with conventional treatments of female ruin—most particularly in "The Ruined Maid," a poem he wrote in 1866 while living in London. His unease with the prevailing literary image of the ruined woman of literature is clear in this wittily ironic dialogue between a laconic prostitute named 'Melia and a friend out of 'Melia's respectable rural past, an amusingly wide-eyed country girl who does most of the talking:

> 'O 'Melia, my dear, this does everything crown!
> Who would have supposed I should meet you in town?
> And whence such fair garments, such prosperi-ty?'—
> 'O didn't you know I'd been ruined?' said she.
>
> —'You left us in tatters, without shoes or socks,
> Tired of digging potatoes, and spudding up docks;
> And now you've gay bracelets and bright feathers three!'
> 'Yes: that's how we dress when we're ruined,' said she.

—'At home in the barton you said "thee" and "thou,"
And "thik oon," and "thëas oon," and "t'other"; but now
Your talking quite fits 'ee for high compa-ny!'—
'Some polish is gained with one's ruin,' said she.

—'Your hands were like paws then, your face blue and bleak
But now I'm bewitched by your delicate cheek,
And your little shoes fit as on any la-dy!'—
'We never do work when we're ruined,' said she.

—'You used to call home-life a hag-ridden dream,
And you'd sigh, and you'd sock; but at present you seem
To know not of megrims or melancho-ly!'—
'True. One's pretty lively when ruined,' said she.

—'I wish I had feathers, a fine sweeping gown,
And a delicate face, and could strut about Town!'—
'My dear—a raw country girl, such as you be,
Cannot quite expect that. You ain't ruined,' said she.
(*Complete Poems*, 158–59)

"The Ruined Maid" is one of the earliest instances of Hardy's conscious divergence from the shame-filled fallen heroine of nineteenth-century literary convention, and the poem is highly untypical of its time for several reasons. Hardy diverges from and affronts established tastes by creating a dialogue between a prostitute and her respectable friend on the topic of sexual ruin—a topic that Victorian poets seldom if ever offered in the form of dialogue, particularly a dialogue between women. By the late 1860s, then, he was already smashing what in the 1890s he would call "the doll of English fiction."

Hardy makes 'Melia, a onetime rural maid who has become a prosperous, resourceful woman of the streets, a clever ironist, a woman keenly aware that "prosperi-ty" can be the reward of sin, and poverty the wage of virtue. Like the striking heroines in Hardy's fiction mentioned above, 'Melia seeks to improve her lot—her dress, her speech, and her place in society. Like them, she understands the constraints of marrying, of domestic life and its brutalizing labors. Like them, she knows the power of her sexuality, although she is the only character who unabashedly turns that power to the ends of prostitution. She is also the only one who resists self-censure; for Hardy lends 'Melia nothing of Tess's agonizing shame. 'Melia has learned to laugh, somewhat grimly to be sure, at what circumstances have made of her.

In several ways, Hardy's Tess Durbeyfield is 'Melia rewritten. The eldest child of a branch of the defunct but once powerful d'Urberville family, Tess lives in near poverty with her drunken father, her slatternly mother, and a covy of siblings. When her father, John, learns from a garrulous parson that he is a descendant of "the ancient and knightly family of the d'Urbervilles" (13), he falls to fantasizing about recovering that lost greatness, and his imaginings infect his foolish wife Joan as well. When a well-to-do newcomer to the neighborhood bears the name d'Urberville, John and Joan all too willingly send Tess, a sixteen-year-old of precocious sexuality and striking personal beauty, to renew kinship. Their excuse for the visit is to ask for help because the death of the family horse in a bloody accident, for which Tess is at least partially to blame, has taken away the family's livelihood. But at the same time, it is clear that John and Joan Durbeyfield need no compelling reason to use Tess's physical charm to establish a connection with wealth. Like 'Melia, Tess is a kind of commodity: the sexuality of both women is for sale. Whereas 'Melia understands this and exploits it, Tess goes mad when this truth is finally brought home to her. 'Melia's salvation is her apparent freedom from moral considerations; Tess's doom is her shame, her capacity for self-condemnation, her fundamental decency.

Whereas Hardy places the "selling" of 'Melia at the center of a bitter social comedy within which 'Melia exercises a degree of control, he makes Tess the center of a sequence of events whose chief purpose is to illustrate that human suffering is irreparable, beyond correction or remedy. Tess's powerlessness pertains not just to the loss of her virginity but also to the larger events that drive her through her life: the decline of her family from wealth and power to poverty, ignorance, and inconsequence; the displacement of her traditional rural order by the at times demonic energies of industrial progress; the overshadowing of her personal hopes and dreams by the play of cosmic forces that are indifferent to her plight. The Christian deity whose minister refuses to bury Tess's bastard child in hallowed ground, like the sporting deity of pagan origin that Hardy invokes in his parting words about Tess, is uncaring, or malign, or misrepresented by his human agencies.

In important ways, Hardy set aside the moral issues inherent in the spectacle of sexual ruin in order to raise certain aesthetic ones. In doing so he was swerving sharply from the predominantly moral treatment of the question favored by other nineteenth-century novelists. Hardy's originality in *Tess*, what made *Tess* shockingly new for readers in the 1890s, and what makes *Tess*, as novel and as a film, deeply interesting to discerning readers of the 1990s, is his portrayal of his much put-upon heroine as a violent, at times aggressively violent woman, and further, in his making her violence, along with her other defects, the basis of a beauty and pleasure whose definition can sustain imaginative interpretations of the novel.

This beauty of violence, of suffering, of agony unto death—most of all this paradoxical beauty in ugliness sets *Tess* apart from the work of Dickens, Eliot, Scott, Richardson, and even Hawthorne, in its portrayal of the sexual ruin of a woman. In his notes about his writing and in the writing itself, Hardy is consistent in his belief that to live is to suffer. More precisely, to live is to suffer because to live is to know desire, and to know desire is to know the pain of the always unbridgeable gap between desire and its objects. This has been called a sexual pessimism, and, indeed, it is; but if it were only that, readers long ago would have set Hardy aside as just another writer of late nineteenth-century off-center novels and poems. But Hardy's readership continues to grow because, particularly in *Tess*, Hardy weds beauty to ugliness in several of its forms: cruelty, deceit, fatal violence, betrayal. So one ought not be surprised that Hardy's stories and poems are so overwhelmingly gloomy, for as Hardy himself stated, the province of the artist is precisely "to find the beauty in ugliness."[5] He describes his reason for believing this in a note of 1877: "Since Nature's defects must be looked in the face and transcribed, . . . the *art* in poetry and novel writing . . . lies in making these defects the basis of a hitherto unperceived beauty, by irradiating them with 'the light that never was' on their surface, but is seen to be latent in them by the spiritual eye" (*Life*, 114).

We will have more to say in chapter 7 about this remark. It is worth noting here, however, that in yoking the defective to the beautiful, Hardy requires that his reader think the unthinkable, for while it may be customary to acknowledge the existence of ugliness in all its forms, it is not at all customary to take pleasure in it, and this is so because the ugly, aesthetically and morally, usually disgusts, repels, and terrifies. In marrying defect and cruelty to beauty, Hardy is not simply dumping traditional pieties or cultivating sadism, though both these things probably play a part; on the contrary, he frequently places in the mouth of his powerfully speculative narrator denunciations of the same forms of pain that, at other moments, this same narrator (in a different mood and voice) serenades.

This narrative shifting between detached narrator and moralizing narrator, the result of Hardy's ironic sense of things, enables him—to cite just two examples—to condemn Alec's violation of Tess and then Angel's abandonment of the resurging Tess at the same time he lyricizes the setting and operation of Alec's destructive lust and Angel's equally destructive fastidiousness. In thus denying his reader an easy response to Tess's pain, that is, a response in either aesthetic ("it is ugly") or moral ("it is wrong") terms, Hardy forces the reader to respond to the irony of things, and therefore to respond indeterminately; or, to use Hardy's favored adjective, impressionistically—anything but dogmatically. Hampering the reader's inclination to deplore the suffering of the innocent and at the same time encouraging the reader to condemn that suffering produces a mixed response—contemplative as well as judgmental—whose chief quality is serenity rooted in awareness of the need to accept, even embrace and take pleasure in, things beyond one's control.

Thus Tess's strongest appeal is not as a virtuous victim—the good person trampled on by circumstances and fate. Tess's unique appeal is the beauty of her defeat. Scott, Eliot, Dickens, to a degree even Hawthorne, define the beauty of their sexually ruined heroines through their real or lost purity, humility, patience, kindness, tender intelligence, or childlikeness. But these heroines are beautiful (in person, heart, and mind) apart from their suffering. Hardy, as radical ironist, makes Tess's beauty part and parcel of her suffering, as if the beauty that is in and about her cannot manifest itself except in the company of what tortures her. This new beauty, this beauty in ugliness, is found not just in her often patient or forgiving responses to pain but also in her visceral experience of pain; there is beauty in her suffering at the same time there is terror in it. Her suffering attracts at the same time that it repels, or better, it attracts because it repels.

Hardy colors Tess's misery with beauty, her beauty with misery, because he chooses not to depict her as simply a victim. Unlike the submissive, passive victims of conventional ruined maiden novels, Tess is willing to oppose and attack her male oppressors and to assume male roles. Hardy also makes her capable of ruthless self-torture. Her readiness to fight back, to do violence to others and to herself, is, Hardy implies, one result of her social anomalousness. Though a young woman of the countryside, she has received enough formal education to know the society beyond her village, and as a result she hates the contempt and patronage that society directs at her and her kind. One notes, for example, that the collapse of her and her family is set in motion when a supercilious clergyman disdainfully informs a tipsy John Durbeyfield of his status as the degraded descendant of a once-powerful family: a learned member of the middle class is here enjoying the fall of one who in former days might have been his social superior and benefactor. Alec's freedoms with Tess, his utter contempt for her personal integrity, and Angel's ambitions for her intellectual and social cultivation are also expressions of class contempt.

But from the earliest descriptions of Tess in the novel, Hardy depicts Tess's arrogant, even aggressive, sense of intrinsic personal superiority to her companions and particularly to her parents—the slatternly Joan and the alcoholic Jack. Out of this social self-consciousness comes Tess's indignation, anger, temper, hatred, and finally, her capacity for inflicting lethal violence, a trait that few heroines of nineteenth-century fiction possess. For example, after she has been violated by Alec, Tess happens upon some game birds that hunters have wounded and left to die. Instead of nursing them back to health, she wrings their necks to end their misery quickly because she has recognized that their plight is worse than hers.

Readers who sympathize too deeply with Hardy's use of his moralizing narrator to excoriate hunting can easily overlook Hardy's recreation in this cruel episode of the aura of Tess's violation by Alec in The Chase. Tess's violent treatment of the birds all too easily replays her own violation by Alec. At least for the moment, she possesses the power of the hunter, or predator, or executioner, or lustful male, or sporting god. Whereas for the most part she struggles near the bottom of the social scale, in this scene she is at least the superior of something, even if it is a wounded bird: moreover she is all too willing to manage its fate. When, later, Alec persists in his attentions to her and insults her beloved (and absent) husband, she draws Alec's blood (and not for the last time) by smashing him across the face with her gauntlet. Still later, after Alec has persuaded her to become his mistress in exchange for supporting her impoverished family, and when he again insults her beloved Angel Clare, Tess takes Alec's life with the thrust of a table knife. For all her tenderness, for all her beauty, for all her purity Tess is a killer—of the wounded birds, of the man who has ruined her, and, as we shall see in chapter 9, of the various creatures of the field who have been entrapped by the work of the harvest.

This heroine whom Hardy endows with surpassing beauty—in look, form, voice, and spirit—retaliates, violently and bloodily, and to no useful end, because she is arrested for murder then hung by the neck on a scaffold at Wintoncester. Tess is violated (by history, by family, by Alec, by Angel), and she responds with violence and in turn is finally, lethally violated. Yet she is also a loving, gentle woman who trusts the man who deceives and violates her, loves the child whose birth out of wedlock brings disgrace to her, devotes herself to the man who marries her, abandons her, then returns too late to her, is always solicitous for the well-being of her family, eager to the end of her life that her sister Liza-Lu know the love of the man Tess worships and must relinquish.

Unlike Greek tragic heroes who fall from greatness because of a tragic flaw, Tess—a woman crushed by poverty, by one man's drunken folly, another man's lust, and a third man's rigid idealism, as well as by her own murderous passion—rises to tragic proportions because she fights against the suffering and oppression meted out to her by an unjust universe. In making his fallen maiden into a heroine and depicting her beauty in suffering Hardy not only violates the tenets of tragedy; he also violates the expectations of his contemporary readers who expect a moral and not an aesthetic response to the deflowering of a maiden.

3

Critical Reception

Although *Tess* is widely regarded as the best of Hardy's Wessex novels, a recurring note in interpretation of the novel from the 1890s to the present is admiration for Hardy's tragic view qualified by displeasure with Hardy's handling of ideas and narrative technique. This divided response began with contemporary reviewers, was echoed by the novelist Henry James in a notorious letter of March 1892, to fellow novelist Robert Louis Stevenson, and was taken up and virtually institutionalized by F. R. Leavis in his study of English fiction, *The Great Tradition* (1948).

Contemporary reviewers, almost to a person, sympathized with Hardy's depiction of the suffering of Tess, and with his portrait of Tess herself, but complained strongly about Hardy's candor in matters of lovemaking, his harsh treatment of Christianity and its clergy, and his notion that Tess is a "pure woman." Henry James found the novel "chock-full of faults and falsities and yet [possessed of] a singular beauty and charm." Leavis excluded Hardy from the company of the greatest writers of English fiction because he purportedly lacked deep certainty of purpose.[6]

Critics have accused Tess of speaking at times with a sophistication that a woman of her station would not likely possess. Also Hardy at times seems too willing to sacrifice probability to expedience, as when Tess's important letter to Angel revealing her past goes astray under a carpet at Talbothays. Angel Clare and Alec d'Urberville in particular are at times one-dimensional rather than interestingly complex characters in a work of fiction. Mary Jacobus complains that in the many changes he made between the manuscript and the last published version Hardy deprived Tess of adequate motivation for some of her most important decisions and actions. Bernard J. Paris complains of Hardy's thematic inconsistency. Yet others, such as Dorothy Van Ghent, complain of the intrusiveness of Hardy's philosophic narrator.

It is relevant to recall that Hardy wrote *Tess* under unusual duress, even for someone as accustomed as he must have been by 1888–91 to writing fiction to meet a deadline. The first one-half of his manuscript was rejected in rather brutal terms by several prospective publishers before he found one who would publish it—but only if he removed the important, and controversial, seduction and baptism scenes. This editorial pressure must have inhibited his work on the second half of the novel, and the hostility of some of the early reviewers could have only increased his caution in the revisions he made for the 1891 and later editions of the novel. He was, after all, making a living by writing novels; and he was notoriously sensitive to expressions of displeasure with his work. It is worth remembering also that only a few years before beginning *Tess,* Hardy had taken on the expense of building an impressive home and setting himself up as something of a country gentleman in his native Dorset. So first Hardy had to write a novel he could sell; then he needed to find a way to salvage the integrity of that novel as a work of art. And he cared passionately about that integrity. Since these salvage efforts took place over some thirty years (1891–1920), it is not surprising that he failed to achieve his original design.

Furthermore, in choosing to work with a story already successfully told by contemporaries of the stature of Sir Walter Scott, Charles Dickens, George Eliot, Nathaniel Hawthorne, and William Makepeace Thackeray, Hardy was hard put to discover original departures. In a remark in his 1892 preface to the fifth and later editions of *Tess* Hardy makes clear the cost of this struggle with his precursors:

> This novel being one wherein the great campaign of the heroine begins after an event in her experience which *has usually been treated as fatal to her part of protagonist, or at least as the virtual ending of her enterprises and hopes* [italics mine], it was quite contrary to avowed conventions that the public should welcome the book and agree with me that there was something more to be said about the shaded side of a well-known catastrophe. But the responsive spirit in which *Tess of the d'Urbervilles* has been received by the readers of England and America would seem to prove that the plan of laying down a story on the lines of tacit opinion, instead of making it to square with the vocal formulae of society, is not altogether a wrong one, *even when exemplified in so unequal and uneven an achievement as the present.* (4; italics mine)

Originality in serious literature is a much-neglected subject and is best understood not as radical novelty but as divergence from or revision of that which already exists. Hardy was a relentless revisionist, not just of his own writing but also of all of those influences that informed his writing—among which his literary precursors are certainly the most important.

Given the circumstances peculiar to the composition of *Tess,* perhaps the single strongest refrain in criticism of the novel has been praise for what might be called its poetry, that is, its qualities of language and organization, the discussion of which does not require strict attention to matters of narrative coherence or thematic consistency. In an influential essay that appeared in 1953 Dorothy Van Ghent, while complaining that Hardy imposes "elements resistant to aesthetic cohesion," praises Hardy for discovering the symbolic event (the death of the Durbeyfield horse) that has "the natural 'grain' of concrete fact" and irrefutable experience.[7] Similarly, in his widely cited "Colour and Movement in Hardy's *Tess of the d'Urbervilles*" (1968), Tony Tanner describes Tess's destiny as "a cumulation of visible omens"[8] in the forms of images of light, redness, verticality and horizontality, and motion. Tanner praises Hardy's use of "visualized passages [to] carry the meaning of the novel" (Tanner, 14), so he is willing to set aside what many have considered Hardy's occasional blunders of plot, characterization, and narration. In "*Tess of the d'Urbervilles*: Repetition as Immanent Design" (1982), J. Hillis Miller, attending to a single important episode, Alec's violation of Tess, discovers manifold repetitions—verbal, thematic, and narrative—in the narrative texture of *Tess*. Setting the criterion for excellence as repetitive symmetry rather than consistency or coherence, Miller contends that *Tess* is not a flawed but an interestingly indeterminate work of narrative art.[9]

Since the late 1970s, feminist critics have faced squarely what has always been a strong factor in Hardy's claim to greatness as a novelist: his discerning but problematic portrayal of women. Actually, feminist critics have cultivated topics that deeply interested Hardy's earliest readers: the prominence of women in Hardy's fiction and Hardy's clear determination to portray women in a way that diverged from that of Dickens, Eliot, Thackeray, and Meredith. He accomplished this by attending to the reality of women's sexuality, aspirations, and intelligence, as well as the anguish that accompanies their frequently thwarted desires to be heard. Hardy went about this quite consciously, as he implies in a letter of December 1891: "Ever since I began to write . . . I have felt that the doll of English fiction must be demolished, if England is to have a school of fiction at all."[10]

Though most feminist commentators on *Tess* acknowledge that there is a degree of unconventionality in Hardy's depiction of women, they differ about his success in portraying women realistically. In "Thomas Hardy: The Man Who 'Liked' Women" (1982), Mary Childers describes contradictions in Hardy's portrayal of women. Penny Boumelha, in *Thomas Hardy and Women: Sexual Ideology and Narrative Form* (1982), analyzes the sometimes mixed results of Hardy's urge to write prose narrative in which he enters sympathetically into the situations of women as well as men. Kristin Brady, in "Tess and Alec: Rape or Seduction?" (1986), draws on the efforts particularly of Mary Jacobus (in "Tess: The Making of a Pure Woman" [1978]), to discover the effects of Hardy's "forced" revisions of *Tess* on his portrayal of his best known heroine. Rosemarie Morgan argues persuasively in *Women and Sexuality in the Novels of Thomas Hardy* (1988) against the view that Tess is a passive victim. Jean Jacques Lecercle ("The Violence of Style in *Tess of the d'Urbervilles* [1989]) views Tess as both victim and perpetrator of violence, but of a violence that is primarily linguistic.

Since the mid-1970s, critics of *Tess*—whatever their intellectual approach—have been aided immeasurably in their reading of Hardy's revisions of *Tess* between 1891 and 1920 by the editorial work of J. T. Laird and Simon Gatrell. Laird's and Gatrell's painstaking efforts will be the basis for the best future readings of *Tess*, particularly for readers who believe that sound criticism proceeds out of awareness of a writer's creative habits.

A Reading

Cross-in-Hand

4

Hardy's Terrible Beauty

Hardy's *Tess of the d'Urbervilles* is now more than one century old. Recently the basis for a widely acclaimed motion picture, Roman Polanski's *Tess* (1979), the novel continues to hold readers because Hardy's story of the devastation of an innocent delves into a familiar and important question—why does a good person suffer?—and enacts that question in disturbingly unfamiliar terms. That is, Hardy explores the question in such a way as to reveal the beauty in Tess's suffering at the same time as he deplores her suffering. This beauty is not simply a result of Hardy's style of rendering Tess's experience, that is, a beauty of manner, effect, or scene; rather, the beauty Hardy portrays derives from the fact that Tess suffers.

Hardy manages this in several ways, most overtly by speaking in two narrative voices: one objective, observing, and attentive to aesthetic effects; the other empathic, evaluative, and given to moral considerations. In the first voice, he speaks of the beauty of suffering, in the second, of the shame and injustice that such suffering should occur. This division of the narration creates a dual perspective that requires that a reader negotiate with the text, reconciling strange pleasure and biting pain in the process of reading about and enjoying the beauty of things normally not enjoyable, normally in fact repulsive. The dual perspective is yet another reason *Tess* continues not just to captivate us but to fascinate us.

Hardy desires that his readers read him with what he calls "generous imaginativeness which shall find in a tale not only all that was put there by the author, put he it never so awkwardly, but which shall find there what was never inserted by him, never foreseen, never contemplated. Sometimes these additions . . . woven around a work of fiction by the intensitive power of the reader's own imagination are the finest part of the scenery."[11] Hardy invites his reader to read creatively, to add to the story of Tess what its author never inserted, foresaw, or contemplated in writing it. Virginia Woolf, an admirer of Hardy's fiction, and still I believe his most balanced critic, contends that "[The Wessex Novels] are never arid; there is always about them a little blur of unconsciousness, that halo of freshness and margin of the unexpressed which often produce the most profound sense of satisfaction. It is as if Hardy himself were not quite aware of what he did, as if his consciousness held more than he could produce, and he left it to his readers to make out his full meaning and to supplement it from their own experience."[12]

This supplementing of what one reads from the content of one's own experience is not so easy as it may seem. We do not merely take that with which we agree in what we read and apply it to events in our own lives. Reading Hardy, for example, in a state of disenchantment with the world and using his supposed pessimism to justify our own disaffection probably does little justice to both the depth of his pessimism and the depth of his skepticism toward that pessimism. One of Hardy's least proclaimed virtues—and perhaps one of his greatest— is his habit of doubting his own doubt, his ability, for example, to declare life meaningless and at the same time acknowledge the meaningfulness of his declaration, and the implication of that meaningfulness for his skepticism.

If *Tess* is a classic, and by that I mean a novel that has continued to speak to our hopes and fears throughout a century of unprecedented horrors and unparalleled glories, that is because we can also speak to *Tess,* can use, to borrow Hardy's odd adjective, our "intensitive" powers of creative imagining to supplement it as we read it. Writing on the centenary of the death of Goethe, the Spanish philosopher José Ortega y Gasset remarked that for him there is but one way to read a classic: to bring the revered text near us by giving it a transfusion of our own blood, by which he means our own collective passions and problems.

It is best, Ortega y Gasset advises, to immerse the classic in our lives. The paradoxical beauty in Tess's suffering can be transfused with our own passions by asking, again and again, some simple and obvious questions: Why does Hardy portray suffering as beautiful? Is he indifferent to the misery to which he subjects Tess? Does he take perverse pleasure, as some critics suggest, in torturing, so to speak, his female protagonist? Hardy's divided narration in *Tess* implies otherwise; for his divided narration is a gesture of sympathy toward Tess at the same time that it is a record of the beauty in her suffering. But how, one wonders, can suffering be a thing of beauty? It can, Hardy implies, if one can suspend the conventional notion of beauty (as that which attracts and pleases, particularly by its appearance or form) long enough to see that one's view of beauty is relative to one's sense of human possibility, which in turn depends on one's cultural circumstances. Hardy recognizes the importance of these skeptical questions, because he—always doubting his doubts—raises doubts about beauty in ugliness in his portrayal of Angel Clare (discussed in Chapter 12), and in doing so implants within his text a powerful contradiction to his notion that beauty dwells in the ugliness of Tess's suffering.

Hardy makes evident his taste for the so-called ugly throughout his novels and poems in his patient, sometimes appallingly patient, interest in death and loss, disappointment and failure; but he reveals this propensity most fully for the first time in *The Return of the Native* (1878), the first of his great tragic novels. In the opening chapter of *Return of the Native* Hardy writes, in a grave philosophic manner, that within the dark, even sinister, contours of Egdon Heath, on which he locates all the novel's important events, dwells a new beauty that displaces the merely scenic beauty of landscape as it is conventionally described. This new beauty exists, he argues, because "human souls . . . find themselves in closer and closer harmony with external things wearing a sombreness distasteful to our race when it was young."[13] In other words, as humanity grows older it must develop a taste for the beauty of "sombreness" because humanity is becoming more and more intimate with "external things" that are shadowy, dark, gloomy, and obscure. Judging from *Return of the Native* and *Tess,* what Hardy means by "external things" can be described in one word: loss—loss of innocence, loss of youthful idealism and energy (whether in the individual or the race), loss of life itself. Hardy's people always end up worse than when they begin, seared by experience, dully adult, or dead; and they end thus because for them living is almost always losing and failing. It is as if Hardy, seeing the pervasiveness of loss, faces that inevitability by endowing it with beauty and thus making it a source of pleasure.

Perhaps a new word is in order for the fusion Hardy effects: *beaugly,* with its variants *beaugliness* and *beaugliful,* admittedly makeshift, is a word that denotes Hardy's estranged vision of things in his fiction and poetry. Hardy's estrangement manifests itself as a new kind of beauty in this passage from the opening chapter of *Return of the Native*:

> Fair prospects [that is, landscapes] wed happily with fair times; but alas, if times be not fair! Men have oftener suffered from the mockery of a place too smiling for their reason than from the oppression of surroundings oversadly tinged. Haggard Egdon [Heath] appealed to a subtler and scarcer instinct, to a more recently learned emotion, than that which responds to the sort of beauty called charming and fair.
>
> Indeed, it is a question if the exclusive reign of this orthodox beauty is not approaching its last quarter. . . . The time seems near, if it has not actually arrived, when the chastened sublimity of a moor, a sea, or a mountain will be all of nature that is absolutely in keeping with the moods of the more thinking among mankind. (*Return,* 34)

What is this rare human instinct or emotion in thoughtful men and women, recent in origin and "oversadly tinged," that must set aside "the sort of beauty called charming and fair" in favor of a beauty of "chastened sublimity"? Hardy does not say.

Hardy seems to be justifying or explaining the ways of God to men and women, but he explains God's ways aesthetically rather than conceptually. For example, Hardy suggests not only that Tess suffers because God is malicious, foolish, blind, or sleeping, but also that Tess's suffering because of God's ineptness is a thing of beauty because it is inevitable, a thing of beauty because suffering is a fact of her and of all human lives. If one observes a group of persons attempting to come to terms with the death of a loved one, it is not unusual to see them attribute beauty to otherwise ordinary, even commonplace, things associated with the deceased. I had occasion recently to be at the deathbed of an aged relative. Her spouse of sixty years stood beside me, touching her cold, discolored cheeks and hands, murmuring "You're so beautiful, so beautiful, so beautiful." To me, she was a horror, swollen, motionless, unnatural in her color, alive at the behest of plastic and metal appendages, all but unrecognizable as the considerate and loving wife he had known when she lived. Her husband saw beauty where I saw not just death, but death's bland ugliness. Hardy frequently places the reader of *Tess* in sight of an extremity of being comparable to that of the observer of the grieving husband; and he does this by painting her circumstances in negatively beautiful colors, at the same time he registers the shame, the injustice of her suffering.

One finds Hardy depicting the beauty of ugliness throughout *Tess,* but nowhere more explicitly, or aptly, than in the landscape he paints from Tess's experience in the opening paragraphs of Phase the Second (entitled "Maiden No More"). The Tess we meet returning from Marlott in dejection and self-hatred is a different Tess than the innocent girl who had left the village a few weeks earlier. Having remained in Alec's company after he raped her—presumably she had the hope that he would marry her—she has to some degree participated in her own ruin. But she is not simply the conventional ruined maid of stories and paintings, fleeing in horror from her ruin. Gazing over the familiar valley where she had known the simplicities of her childhood, she finds she views Blakemore Vale differently than before she lost her innocence. Hardy's detached, observing narrator speaks: "It was always beautiful from here; it was terribly beautiful to Tess to-day, for since her eyes last fell upon it she had learnt that the serpent hisses where the sweet birds sing, and her views of life had been totally changed for her by the lesson. Verily another girl than the simple one she had been at home was she who, bowed by thought, stood still here, and turned to look behind her. She could not bear to look forward into the Vale."[14]

How a "terrible beauty" can supplant the "always beautiful" is illuminated in William Butler Yeats's poem "Easter, 1916," in which "a terrible beauty is born" to the poet because of the meaningless deaths of four soldiers fighting in a civil war.[15] Yeats's appeal, like Hardy's, is to a beauty that is unorthodox because it is derived from what is conventionally displeasing, in Yeats's case, from violent death in war. For Yeats, the beauty in lethal violence is beyond human comprehension; so it is not the poet's but "Heaven's part" to judge whether it was wise for the dead rebels to have sacrificed so much.

Hardy's comment on the violated Tess, like Yeats's song to the dead rebels, points to the irreparable loss that is at the root of terrible beauty: a beauty that terrifies at the same time that it pleases us because it emanates from sources beyond our reach, our control, and our comprehension. The unorthodox beauty of the dead warriors when seen through the eyes of the poet approaches the beauty that Tess beholds as she gazes, after her irretrievable loss, over the valley of her innocent childhood.

This blending of incongruous words or ideas is an oxymoron, but there is no term for Hardy's insistence that the ugly is beautiful, the beautiful ugly. Actually, by forging this particular opposition, Hardy reaches toward what the eighteenth-century philosopher Edmund Burke called "the Sublime," by which he meant "whatever is in any sort terrible," and in being terrible "is productive of the strongest emotion which the mind is capable of feeling."[16] Whereas Burke had distinguished sharply between the sublime ("whatever is qualified to cause terror") and the beautiful ("whatever produces . . . positive and original pleasure") (Burke, 131), Hardy, by way of diverging from

Burke, whom he read and admired, fuses the sublime and the beautiful; that is, for Hardy terror and pleasure, respectively, are one and the same.

Like Yeats in "Easter, 1916," Hardy's part is to "murmur name upon name," to "write it out," again and again. And so Hardy's readers must infer the beaugly out of their own passions and problems, and in inferring, create a name for, an understanding of, the unorthodox marriage of beauty and ugliness that is part of the life and death of Tess Durbeyfield.

5

Death by Starlight

The beaugly course of Tess Durbeyfield's life is determined by—of all things—the violent and bloody death of a horse. In the course of the novel, Hardy builds several parallels between the death of the Durbeyfields' beast of burden and the disgrace and death of their daughter. Not only does this critical event set in motion the events that lead directly to Tess's death; Hardy also creates in this episode his first vision of the beaugly, setting up visual and thematic currents that run through the rest of the novel.

This determinative event occurs in chapter 4, where Hardy tells in vivid detail of the death of Prince, the Durbeyfield nag, in a pool of his own blood in the soft, dim light of dawn, with Tess at his reins in a half-sleeping state, her tiny brother Abraham at her side. Death comes to Prince when his breast is gored by the shaft of another horse-drawn cart. The collision is clearly the fault of Tess—the result of her sleepily driving her cart on the wrong side of the road from Marlott to Casterbridge with a load of honey for market.

> A sudden jerk shook her in her seat, and Tess awoke from the sleep into which she . . . had fallen. . . .

Death by Starlight

A hollow groan, unlike anything she had ever heard in her life, came from the front, followed by a shout of 'Hoi, there!' . . .

Something terrible had happened. The harness was entangled with an object which blocked the way.

In consternation Tess jumped down, and discovered the dreadful truth. The groan had proceeded from her father's poor horse Prince. The morning mail-cart, with its two noiseless wheels, speeding along these lanes like an arrow, as it always did, had driven into her slow and unlighted equipage. The pointed shaft of the cart had entered the breast of the unhappy Prince like a sword; and from the wound his life's blood was spouting in a stream, and falling with a hiss into the road.

In her despair Tess sprang forward and put her hand upon the hole, with the only result that she became splashed from face to skirt with the crimson drops. Then she stood hopelessly looking on. Prince also stood firm and motionless as long as he could; till he suddenly sank down in a heap. . . .

Tess stood and waited. The atmosphere turned pale, the birds shook themselves in the hedges, arose, and twittered: the lane showed all its white features, and Tess showed hers, still whiter. The huge pool of blood in front of her was already assuming the iridescence of coagulation; and when the sun rose a hundred prismatic hues were reflected from it. Prince lay alongside still and stark; his eyes half open, the hole in his chest looking scarcely large enough to have let out all that had animated him. (*Tess*, 36–37)

This gruesome event—made more so because Tess's brother, her companion for the journey, must witness the result of her carelessness—does more than decide her life's outcome, or, as critics frequently note, prefigure Alec's violation of her a short time later. In this scene, Hardy for the first time in the novel reveals his departure from convention by conferring beauty, almost ceremonial beauty, on violent death, and the violent death of an animal at that. He makes this change by lyricizing the circumstances of the death, both in the passages that describe the incident and in the paragraphs leading to them.

He does this stylistically: by moving between past perfect and past progressive tenses; by repeating the coordinating conjunction "and" to capture Tess's purely reflexive responses to the catastrophe;

by using analogy (the "white features" of the lane, the "still whiter" features of Tess); and by speaking intermittently in the voice of a detached, serene observer for whom the visual qualities of the bloody spectacle are as interesting as the suffering of the animal and the persons. Hardy's tone here, his complex attitude toward his material, is difficult to describe. There is deep sadness in it, but even more than sadness, there is a laconicism that is actually a reluctance to say all, a resolve perhaps to keep unknown a truth too cruel for human minds.

He displays this peculiar sadness and reserve when his observing, detached narrator describes "the place of the blood-pool" on the evening of the day on which the accident occurs: "[it] was still visible in the middle of the road, though scratched and scraped over by passing vehicles" (37–38). The shimmering blood pool of the morning—strangely beautiful in its radiance—has been travelled over and therefore becomes the darkened blood pool of the evening. That there can be beauty in the former—a puzzling proposition at best—becomes more plausible because of the contrast between the blood of morning and the blood of evening.

In the contrast he captures, briefly but exactly, between the radiance of the pool of blood by morning and the same pool's marred state by evening Hardy draws an analogy to Tess's state before and after her undoing. The comely young woman whom he first placed before us, only one day earlier, wearing the white dress of innocence at a village festival, he now, with shocking abruptness and vividness, baptizes in blood, exposing her helplessness before death and her inability to undo her role in causing death.

Tess's unqualified self-condemnation ("'Tis all my doing—all mine!" [37]), is credible, but this is only one response to the disaster, for Hardy also speaks from two other perspectives, one evaluative and moral, the other descriptive and aesthetic.

When Hardy's sympathetic, moralizing narrator evaluates the accident philosophically, he diminishes Tess's responsibility for the death by allowing that lives on a "blighted" planet such as the Earth are likely to encounter misfortune: children such as Tess and Abraham will have irresponsible parents who will send them to do the work of adults, and in doing that work these unfortunate children will meet with disaster. Yet when Hardy speaks descriptively, that is, aesthetically, he sets aside gloomy speculating in favor of narration in which he is less interested in assigning blame and cursing the gods than in relating the sounds (the horse's "hollow groan," the blood "falling with a hiss"), the colors ("crimson," "a hundred prismatic hues"), even the feel ("a sudden jerk," "put her hand upon the hole . . . [and] became splashed from face to skirt") of violent death (37). And he makes these palpable sensations radiant and rainbowlike, suffused with light, not dark, sinister, repellent, or ugly. Hardy directs attention as much to the visual appeal of the "hundred prismatic hues" glancing off the coagulating blood as to Tess's attempt to save the stricken Prince, and the collision itself. The driver of the other cart is matter-of-factly helpful, his response, and even Tess's response, made to seem less important than what one might call the beauty in the chemistry of the bleeding that accompanies the death.

Hardy makes this event an aesthetic moment, a moment of beauty as well as a moment of gory death in which he can show things taking on a strange serenity, finality, and appeal. It is as if he would suggest that even in the worst events something of value exists, but only if one has the eyes, and the stomach, to perceive it. He prepares the reader for this bizarrerie by placing Tess and her brother "mentally in [an]other world," that is, in "a vague interspace" between dream and reality (34). Because Abraham moves "in a sort of trance" as they travel, he talks about "the strange shapes assumed by the various dark objects against the sky; of this tree that looked like a raging tiger springing from a lair; of that which resembled a giant's head" (34). For the same reason, Tess likens the Earth to a blighted apple hanging from a cosmic stubbard apple tree. Hardy transmutes the dreary spectacle of two poor children in a rickety cart on a dark road into something sublimely appealing when, speaking in the voice of his detached narrator, he describes Abraham making "observations on the stars, whose cold pulses were beating amid the black hollows above, in serene dissociation from these two wisps of human life" (35). Because Tess is so deep in reverie, "the mute procession past her shoulders of trees and hedges became attached to fantastic scenes outside reality, and the occasional heave of the wind became the sigh of some immense sad soul, conterminous with the universe in space, and with history in time" (36). Note that in this last sentence Hardy shifts point of view in mid-sentence, at the verb "sigh," from the detached observer to the sympathetic moralizer who feels the cosmos is sighing in sympathy with Tess and Abraham.

Making things strange by attributing beauty to the conventionally ugly or commonplace involves trespassing, and trespassing, an unwelcome or illicit incursion, is Hardy's frequent tactic for capturing that moment when the ugly, mundane, or horrible becomes somehow pleasing to the eye. But, of course, the ugly is never welcome to the mind—at least not immediately—for the mind battens on familiar things—on memories, expectations, habits. For the reader of this passage to take in Hardy's depiction of "beaugliness" requires abandoning certain expectations. The reader who sees the death of Prince as beautiful has to fuse feelings and values normally kept in separate compartments of the mind. For the reader whose understandable impulse is to describe the bloody bath of Tess as "gross," being asked to regard that death as beautiful seems absurd. But when Hardy chooses to impose on his reader in this way, he is rewriting the old—in this case the old story of the ruin of an innocent—"with added ideas," with, that is, the idea that the ugly is beautiful.[17]

It is helpful to consider this matter in terms of motion and stillness. When he speaks through his moralizing narrator, Hardy invites the reader to move around (in both senses of the phrase) the horse's death and Tess's horror by subjecting the telling of the incident to various questions: Is the event the result of pure misfortune? of Tess's carelessness? of her parents' folly? of the working of cosmic defect? On the other hand, when speaking through the observing narrator, Hardy exacts something quite different: he requires the reader to sit still and to contemplate the incident in a frozen silence in which pattern, color, sound, and touch are of primary importance. The reader is a paralyzed, or traumatized, witness, a person seeing a disaster but unable to do anything about it and unable to remove his or her eyes from the spectacle. Hardy fuses beauty with what usually is beauty's negation in several key episodes throughout *Tess*. Illustrating this recurring coalescence, which is present from the earliest stages of his manuscript, was one of his main aims in writing the novel. In the chapters that follow we will observe the permutations of the beauty in ugliness in five other major episodes in *Tess*: Alec's violation of Tess amidst the dark loveliness of The Chase (chapter 11); Tess's baptism of her dying infant (chapter 14); Tess's impassioned encounter with Angel in the weedy beauty of the garden at Talbothays dairy (chapter 19); Angel's rejection of Tess on their wedding night before the shifting colors of a dying fire (chapters 34–36); and Tess's execution for the murder of Alec (chapter 59). Though striking similarities connect these five episodes, one gains little by merely describing repetitions, for Hardy's originality lies in his power to improvise on the "beaugly."

6

Death's Architecture

Using architectural imagery may seem an odd tactic when one tries to imagine other ways in which Hardy might have displayed beauty in Tess's death by hanging and brought his novel to a close. But the language and perspectives of architecture had been familiar to Hardy since he was a teenager. Before becoming a writer, he had been an architectural draftsman and had directed the restoration of churches. He knew well the idioms of architecture and had a special fondness— evident in his poems as well as in his novels—for the "edificial," for framing the irregular contours of the human figure with the angularities of architectural structures. Hardy set dozens of his poems, and many important episodes in his novels and stories, "in" the horizontals and verticals of an edifice or cluster of edifices: a nuptial chamber, a waiting room at a rail station, a museum, a London apartment, a seaside resort, a eweleaze, or, in the case of the final chapter of *Tess,* the buildings of the fine old city of Wintoncester. To elicit beauty from the scene of Tess's hanging in Wintoncester, and thereby create the beaugly, Hardy imposes one architectural image on another, then imposes this piggybacked image on a landscape.

With this predilection for the edificial in mind, it is worth considering how easily Hardy might have written this scene in wildly, even drippingly, emotional terms. Hardy chooses to write no heart-wrenching and emotional account of Tess's and Angel's last words to each other, nothing of Tess's and Liza-Lu's last words, nothing of the actual spectacle of Tess's hanging, which presumably Angel and Liza-Lu might have witnessed had they wished to do so; nothing about the public spectacle that hangings frequently became in nineteenth-century life and art. Instead we picture Tess's body, the object of closest attention throughout the narrative, lying lifeless, apparently abandoned by its departing husband and sister, the survivors who apparently will not even see it to its grave and burial—at least there is no mention of these things.

Hardy chose to avoid a coffin- or grave-side scene, a situation he had exploited in *Far from the Madding Crowd* (chapter 43), where Troy, the seducer of pathetic Fanny Robin, embraces her encoffined corpse in the presence of his outraged wife. In the final chapter of *Tess*, Tess is soon to be hanged, but her husband and her beloved sister are not at her side. Angel and Liza-Lu simply pause to look back on Wintoncester, presumably the city of their deepest sorrow. As we know, Hardy had granted Tess's unfortunate horse Prince a funeral, complete with wailing children and Tess, who thinks she is the horse's murderess (38).

Hardy uses both voices—the guide's and the sympathizer's—to prevent Angel's and Liza-Lu's sorrow from overpowering the reader's perception of the beaugly scene in Wintoncester. As in his depiction of the death of Prince in an iridescent pool of blood over 50 chapters earlier, Hardy again blocks emotional response, this time by attending more to the architectural beauty of the spectacle that frames Tess's death than to the feelings it provokes. First the detached narrator describes the city as a travel guide might:

> The city of Wintoncester—that fine old city, aforetime capital of Wessex—lay amidst its convex and concave downlands in all the brightness and warmth of a July morning. The gabled brick, tile, and freestone houses had almost dried off for the season their integ-

ument of lichen, the streams in the meadows were low, and in the sloping High-street, from the West Gateway to the medieval cross, and from the medieval cross to the bridge, that leisurely dusting and sweeping was in progress which usually ushers in an old-fashioned market-day. (383)

Hardy's second voice is that of a sympathetic onlooker who is more engaged in the suffering taking place before his eyes: "Up [the] road from the precincts of the city two persons were walking rapidly, as if unconscious of the trying ascent—unconscious through preoccupation, and not through buoyancy. . . . They seemed anxious to get out of sight of the houses and of their kind, and this road appeared to offer the quickest means of doing so. Though they were young they walked with bowed heads, which gait of grief the sun's rays smiled on pitilessly" (383).

Instead of entering into the feelings of these sad survivors walking their "gait of grief," with the help of an allusion to a painting by Giotto Hardy's sympathetic narrator attends to their appearance only: "Their pale faces seemed to have shrunk to half their natural size; they moved on hand in hand, and never spoke a word, the drooping of their heads being that of Giotto's Two Apostles" (383). At the sound of the city's clocks striking the hour of eight, this same narrative voice informs us, the two, "impelled by a force that seemed to overrule their will suddenly stood still, turned, looked back at the skyline and waited in paralyzed suspense" (383).

His arrangement of the architectural features of the city surrounding the execution that is never described teases the reader into imagining her death in all its beaugliness. Tess will drop to her death when the clocks of Wintoncester strike the hour of eight from the towers of various buildings. Hardy prepares the reader for realizing that Tess is dead by interposing two superb paragraphs, the third and fourth paragraphs from the end of the novel, between the cacophony of sounding bells and the raising, a few minutes after eight, of a black flag from the cornice of "an ugly flat-topped octagonal tower" (384). In these two paragraphs Hardy uses his two narrative voices as if they were one—the voice of the sympathetic moralizer on Tess's fate shares the telling with the voice of the travel guide.

The reader sees what Angel and Liza-Lu see: the cathedral tower, the spire of St. Thomas's, the college tower, and "the tower and gables of the ancient hospice, where to this day the pilgrim may receive his dole of bread and ale" (384). This prospect is conventionally beautiful because of the shapes it contains and perhaps because some of the buildings host institutions of charity and learning. Hardy reinforces this beauty by describing a radiant, sunlit scene: "Behind the city swept the rotund upland of St Catherine's Hill, further off, landscape beyond landscape, till the horizon was lost in the radiance of the sun hanging above it" (384). But along with this combination of medieval architecture and pastoral contours, Hardy uses his narrator—speaking as both guide and moralist—to describe the confounding and un-masking of this orthodox beauty. Before the eyes of Angel and Liza-Lu and in front of the sun-backed Gothic-pastoral scene, the reader, with them, sees

> a large red-brick building, with level grey roofs, and rows of short barred windows bespeaking captivity—the whole contrasting greatly by its formalism with the quaint irregularities of the Gothic erections. . . . The wicket from which the pair had lately emerged was in the wall of this structure. From the middle of the [large red-brick] building an ugly flat-topped octagonal tower ascended against the east horizon, and viewed from this spot, on its shady side and against the light, it seemed the one blot on the city's beauty. Yet it was with this blot, and not with the beauty, that the two gazers were concerned. (384)

Whereas Angel and Liza-Lu see "the blot" and not "the beauty" because their beloved Tess has been hanged within the ugly tower, the reader—responding to Hardy's arrangement of the scene—sees the conventional beauty through the blot, the blot against that same beauty. To use Hardy's architectural jargon, the scene combines the "formalism" of the modern red brick prison and its swinging victim in juxtaposition with the "irregularities" of the medieval structures.

The suspended form of Tess, itself irregular and beautiful, is captive—legally, physically, and aesthetically—within the angularities of the modern edifice. This is Hardy's "edificial" vision of the beaugly.

Hardy uses both narrative voices to comment on these interpenetrative oppositions. The guide, detached and dry-eyed, notes: "Upon the cornice of the tower a tall staff was fixed. Their eyes were rivetted on it. A few minutes after the hour had struck something moved slowly up the staff, and extended itself upon the breeze. It was a black flag" (384). The moral advocate, always suspended between things as they are and things as they should be, speaks one of the more famous lines of British fiction: "'Justice' was done, and the President of the Immortals (in Aeschylean phrase) had ended his sport with Tess" (384).

This sentence offended certain contemporary readers because Hardy seemed to be denying the existence of a loving God, the God of orthodox Christians, the God whose monuments are prominent among those buildings Hardy describes in his final scene. Hardy was, indeed, denying God's existence, but he was not merely arguing theology; he was creating an estranged perspective on Tess's career by setting a distant perspective from heaven alongside the close at hand, anesthetized perspective of Angel and Liza-Lu.

Hardy remarked in his preface to the fifth edition of *Tess* that he "intended" his novel "to be neither didactic nor aggressive, but in the scenic parts to be representative simply, and in the contemplative to be oftener charged with impressions than with convictions" (4). In truth, Hardy writes both aggressively (as when he invokes the pagan deity) and representatively (as when he eschews depicting emotion in favor of describing spectacle). But Hardy is also aggressive in his determination to use an old plot in a different way and to create the conditions for collapsing conventional categories of response, engaging in what a theorist of literary creating might call oppositional thinking: the superimposing of one visual image upon another (as in the opening of the chapter, the piggybacked architectural image imposed on the landscape); the thinking of contradictory thoughts simultaneously (beauty/ugliness, Christian charity/legalized killing). By forcing one idea or image onto the mental terrain normally occupied by another, contradictory, idea or image Hardy creates an adequate, though not perfect, allusion to Tess's victimhood: her condition as one trespassed upon, violated, deceived, abandoned, taken into captivity, and hanged.

In the final scene Hardy's aggressive substitution of beauty in ugliness for something more orthodox and more familiar—beauty in loving grief or ugliness in loss—echoes without repeating earlier moments of "beaugliness" in the novel: the death of Prince, Alec's violation of Tess, Tess's midnight baptism of her dying son, Angel's encounter with Tess in a weedy garden, and Angel's desertion of Tess on their wedding night.

7

Beauty Dwells Where Defect Lives

Hardy's unorthodox notion that in art, as in life, beauty can dwell with ugliness is really a talent for producing a species of the grotesque, for exacting of his readers a mixture of thoughts and feelings that at once disturb and please. A kind of grotesquerie is the result of Hardy's mingling scenic tranquility, harmony, and visual obscurity with death, blood, fear, cruelty, and other horrible events. Hardy remarked so frequently on such blendings outside his novels that it is worth examining some of his remarks before going on to other instances of his version of the grotesque, or the beaugly, in *Tess*.

As briefly noted earlier, Hardy made a particularly illuminating observation on beaugliness in literary art in 1877, some fifteen years before he wrote *Tess*:

> There is enough poetry in what is left [in life], after all the false romance has been abstracted, to make a sweet pattern. . . . So, then, if Nature's defects must be looked in the face and transcribed, whence arises the *art* in poetry and novel writing? which must certainly show art, or it becomes merely mechanical reporting. I think the art lies in making these defects the basis of a hitherto unperceived beauty, by irradiating them with "the light that never was"

on their surface, but is seen to be latent in them by the spiritual eye.
(*Life*, 114)

Hardy assumes here that people normally perceive themselves and their world through a cloud of "false romance," through rose-colored glasses, so to speak; not because people are perverse, but because survival requires such delusion. Although the writer sees through this blinding mist (of myth, belief, emotion, philosophy, ideology, or egotism), enough "poetry," by which Hardy simply means "mystery" or "the unseen," remains for the writer to make of it "a sweet pattern." According to Hardy, beneath these distortions in human perception exists bedrock reality, "Nature's defects" in all their mystery—in Tess's case, a marred genealogy, irresponsible parents, troubled economic times, social inequities, the ever-present cosmic misworking that produces misfortune.

Hardy's writer possesses something like a transformative x-ray vision—a power to see ever-present defective reality and to make that ugly reality beautiful in some original way by "irradiating" it with "light that never was," that is, with a unique way of seeing and feeling, and of using language. When Hardy speaks of irradiating the ugly, he can mean it almost literally—lighting up the ugly, irradiating or iridescing it, and thereby exposing its masked beauties. Hardy exposes the ugliness of defect, the tumor beneath the apparently healthy flesh; then he makes that tumorous reality "the basis of a hitherto unperceived beauty."

This last phrase is worth pausing over because in it Hardy allows that he can only approximate his aim and that he can only achieve this approximation with the help of his reader, someone with whom to cooperate in the unveiling of a beauty hitherto unperceived. Though he can make defect the basis of a new beauty, Hardy knows he cannot literally transform defect into beauty, cannot make a silk purse of a sow's ear, so to speak. His accomplishment is always virtual, never actual, but he is so skillful in the rendering as to create the illusion of actuality. Equally important, Hardy does not consider novelty something radically new, or wholly unprecedented, but something hitherto unperceived—novelty for Hardy is divergence from something already existing rather than something original. This is Hardy's intelligence as artist and thinker, his sense of the limits of human intellect.

A short time after writing down the remarks quoted above, Hardy restated and expanded them, this time with the aid of several examples: a painting by the late nineteenth-century Italian artist Giovanni Boldini, a painting by the seventeenth-century Dutch artist Meindert Hobbema, and, most interestingly and even oddly, a drinking mug that once belonged to a beloved relative:

> The method of Boldini, the painter of "The Morning Walk" in the French Gallery . . . (a young lady beside an ugly blank wall on an ugly highway)—of Hobbema, in his view of a road with formal lopped trees and flat tame scenery—is that of infusing emotion into the baldest external objects either by the presence of a human figure among them, or by mark of some human connections with them.
>
> This accords with my feeling . . . that the beauty of association is entirely superior to the beauty of aspect, and a beloved relative's old battered tankard to the finest Greek vase. Paradoxically put, it is to see the beauty in ugliness. (*Life* 120–21)

In the last two sentences, Hardy acknowledges two kinds of beauty: the beauty of form or design, as in the symmetry of a Greek vase; and the beauty of association, as in the traces left by hand and lip on a relative's well-used drinking mug. These two kinds of beauty are compatible with the practice of the painters Boldini and Hobbema, who alter the ugliness of a scene by including some "mark of . . . human connections." Beauty of association, which is a beauty of affect rather than of form or design, exists only because a viewer projects feeling for a person onto the inanimate object, in this case a battered implement, or an ugly wall on an equally ugly highway, thereby humanizing that object in a private way, lending it a meaning it would probably not possess for another person. "An object or mark raised or made by a man on a scene," Hardy believed, "is worth ten times any such formed by unconscious Nature. Hence mists, and mountains are unimportant beside the wear on a threshold, or the print of a hand" (*Life*, 116).

Beauty Dwells Where Defect Lives

The "wear [of feet] on a threshold, or the print of a hand" are valued over "unconscious Nature" because Hardy associates Nature with beauty of aspect, design, or scene. In a similar way, Hardy believed the "human interest in an edifice ranks before its architectural interest, however great the latter may be" because "life, after all, is more than art, and that which appealed to us in the (may be) clumsy outlines of some structure which had been looked at and entered by a dozen generations of ancestors outweighs the more subtle recognition, if any, of architectural qualities (*Personal Writings*, 207, 215). For Hardy, such marks of human trespass on Nature or on a building form the basis for a new beauty: "clouds, mists, and mountains" formed by "unconscious Nature" are as nothing beside signs of the human on the nonhuman; the purely aesthetic aspects of a building are as nothing beside the memorial or associative aspects of it.

Hardy's view runs strongly counter to our sentimental view, fairly recent in origin, that a human presence in Nature is always an imposition or a blight. Many of us believe that natural beauty is best perceived in so-called pristine or unspoiled nature, and so we labor to set aside tracts of so-called virgin nature, as if isolating such a tract were not itself an intrusion. But Hardy was too canny to think of nature as something that exists apart from the human, or that the human is something contemplatable apart from nature, for he saw human nature as continuous with so-called nonhuman nature, not as something separate from and inferior, or superior, to it.

Hardy's valuing the human over the larger order that might be said to frame it is consistent with his wish to show beauty in ugliness. Hardy believed that human life is unavoidably out of harmony with the orders that encompass its movements; therefore one's existence, when judged by the standards of the universe, is inescapably defective, imperfect, inadequate. Humankind is vindicated when the artist exhibits the beauty in the deficiencies of human life and exposes the tragedy of the hopeless struggle to beat against the restraints of fate. As we shall see in chapter 12, because Angel Clare cannot see beauty in Tess's defects, cannot embrace the tragic, and because he sees only ugliness in her sexual impurity, he rejects her humanity, and thus her furious struggle to overcome her inescapable defects.

Hardy's notion that the human enhances the nonhuman is also important to enjoying the powerful episodes in *Tess* in which he portrays Tess moving alone across a landscape, particularly a landscape such as that at Flintcomb-Ash, that barren highland where Tess labors in the bitter cold of winter, wondering if Angel Clare will ever return to her. Here Hardy puts to work in vivid terms his notion that a human presence in a baldly natural scene beautifies that scene. Tess travels to Flintcomb out of desperation; she has exhausted the funds Angel had given her upon his departure for Brazil and must now fend for herself. She rambles with "something of the habitude of the wild animal," sheds her more fashionable clothes for "the wrapper of a field-woman," and because passing men comment on her beauty, makes herself ugly by snipping off her eyebrows and wrapping her head in a bandana, giving herself the appearance of a person with a toothache (269–72). In this state of self-inflicted ugliness, she arrives at Flintcomb, where "the air was dry and cold," the roads "white and dusty" (273), and where a farmhouse "was almost sublime in its dreariness" (275). Hardy takes great pains to lend this setting a Boldini-like effect ("a young lady beside an ugly blank wall on an ugly highway"):

> Towards the second evening she [Tess] reached the irregular chalk tableland or plateau, bosomed with semi-globular tumuli—as if Cybele the Many-breasted [Phrygian goddess of fertility] were supinely extended there—which stretched between the valley of her birth and the valley of her love. . . . There were few trees, or none, those that would have grown in the hedges being mercilessly plashed down with the quickset [woven into hedges] by the tenant-farmers, the natural enemies of tree, bush, and brake. . . . The swede-field, in which she and her companion were set hacking, was a stretch of a hundred odd acres, in one patch, on the highest ground of the farm, rising above stony lanchets . . . —the outcrop of siliceous veins in the chalk formation, composed of myriads of loose white flints in bulbous, cusped, and phallic shapes. . . . Every leaf of the vegetable having already been consumed the whole field was in colour a desolate drab; it was complexion without features, as if a face from chin to brow should be only an expanse of skin. The sky wore, in another colour, the same likeness; a white vacuity of countenance

with the lineaments gone. So these two upper and nether visages confronted each other, all day long the white face looking down on the brown face, and the brown face looking up at the white face, without anything standing between them but the two girls crawling over the surface of the former like flies. (273, 277)

In the "desolate drab" of this setting, the presence of Tess (and Marian, Tess's companion from Talbothays days) infuses human emotion, and therefore infuses beauty, into a scene otherwise thoroughly ugly in texture and appearance. Marian and Tess talk of their happier days at Talbothays; Marian keeps herself warm by sipping from "a pint bottle corked with a white rag" (278) and makes a joke about the phallic shape of the flints lying on the frozen ground. In spite of the bitter cold "the young women were fairly cheerful" (281). Hardy, in the language of his aesthetic narrator, even associates the two women on the frozen landscape with "some early Italian conception of the two Marys" (277).

Although Hardy does not achieve here a perfect illustration of beaugliness, he clearly infuses emotion into a bleak landscape by placing human figures in it and creating thereby a beauty of association, or feeling, that is more than a beauty of aspect or scene. And, exceeding his "theory" in his practice here, he heightens this beauty of human association by lending elements of pure fantasy to the scene, making it as coldly alien as possible, thereby increasing the distance between the human presence in and the bald external elements of the scene.

[The winter] came on in stealthy and measured glides like the moves of a chess-player. One morning the few lonely trees and the thorns of the hedgerows appeared as if they had put off a vegetable for an animal integument. Every twig was covered with a white nap as of fur grown from the rind during the night, giving it four times its usual stoutness; the whole bush or tree forming a staring sketch in white lines on the mournful grey of the sky and horizon. . . .

. . . [S]trange birds from behind the north pole began to arrive silently on the upland of Flintcomb-Ash; gaunt spectral creatures with tragical eyes—eyes which had witnessed scenes of cataclysmal horror in inaccessible polar regions, of a magnitude such as no human being had ever conceived, in curdling temperatures that no man could endure; which had beheld the crash of icebergs and the slide of snow-hills by the shooting lights of the Aurora; been half blinded by the whirl of colossal storms and terraqueous distortions; and retained the expression of feature that such scenes had engendered. (279–80)

Here the human presences contend with not just baldly external presences of wintery nature but also with something weirdly animate, even monstrous, in nature: trees with the furriness of animals, birds with a superhuman experience. The earth on which Tess and Marian work is a featureless brown face staring upward at the featureless white face of the sky; and the women are flies crawling about on the vacant brown face. Things of nature mutate in the scene, defying description or categorization; at the same time, the two women work, feel, think, remember, even laugh. Hardy uses alliteration to bring out the beauty in an ugly landscape: "whales and white bears," "the snow . . . that licked the land," "the flossy fields," "hedges that acted as strainers rather than screens" (280–81). The suggestion of something visible yet beyond the categories of color is a fitting metaphor for something that is thinkable yet beyond the categories of thought; such is Hardy's characterization of Tess's beauty—something that requires that Hardy look for beauty in normally unbeautiful places and situations.

8

The Goring of Tess

In the critical scene in which Hardy conveys Alec's violation of Tess without really describing it, Hardy chose to repeat several elements of the episode in which the horse Prince was gored by the shaft of the mail cart. Because Tess's rape proves as fatal as Prince's wound, Hardy surrounds her rape and its aftermath with words, events, and settings that evoke a new but reminiscent sense of the beaugly.

As in the earlier scene, Hardy places Tess on a journey with a male companion, though this time she is on a fine horse, riding double with the scheming Alec rather than sitting beside an innocent brother in a dilapidated cart behind a creeping nag. Again Hardy sets his scene in half-light, in this case the light of late evening rather than early morning. It is worth noting, given Hardy's use of light to evoke the beaugly, that Hardy makes a distinction between the half-light of dawn and the half-light of dusk: "The gray half-tones of daybreak are not the grey half-tones of the day's close, though the degree of their shade may be the same. In the twilight of the morning, light seems active, darkness passive; in the twilight of evening it is the darkness which is active and crescent, and the light which is the drowsy reverse" (134). Again events occur semi-visibly, not just in darkness, but in a misty darkness that corresponds to Tess's semi-conscious mental state, her "moment of oblivion." In both instances Tess is less than fully alert when on the brink of an event full of consequence for her future. And in both cases she is brought to consciousness by a trespass of violent penetration—by the thrust of the mail cart's pointed shaft into the breast of Prince, by Alec's forcing himself on her.

Alec's violation of Tess has been called various things: seduction, rape, appropriation. Yet when seen as a reenactment of the collision on the road to Casterbridge, it takes on lineaments of something else, a goring, that is, a piercing or wounding as if by a horned animal. It differs from the collision between horses and carts because it is no accident. Alec's violation of Tess is premeditated, as is suggested by "the darkness that is active and crescent," and—in the view of both Tess and Angel—the violation is irreversible. The lost horse is replaced (by Alec, ironically, immediately before he violates Tess in The Chase), but there is no restoring Tess's lost virginity. Alec tries to restore her respectability by offering marriage, but respectability is not maiden-head. It is this complete loss that torments Tess and that moves Angel to reject her later in the novel. Hardy spurns the notion that such loss is irrecoverable when he subtitles the novel "A Pure Woman" and not "A Pure Maid." Hardy suggests Tess could undo her sense of loss were she able to set aside her shame, but she loves Angel so deeply that she obeys his censorious view of her, so she cannot do so. And finally, Alec's goring of Tess is as fatal as the goring of the family horse; the "trespass" into both Prince and Tess destroys them. But it is one thing for Hardy to depict the beauty in ugliness of the accidental goring of a horse and quite another for him to exhibit beauty in the rape of a virgin. Here Hardy places himself, and his reader, on difficult ground.

As always, in these strangely transmissive moments Hardy distances us from the emotional intensity of the incident by using two voices: the detached observer who sees terrible beauty and the moralizing observer who sympathizes with the human tragedy. Here is Hardy's indignant moral narrator, reflecting on Tess's undoing: "But, might some say, where was Tess's guardian angel? where was the Providence of her simple faith? Perhaps, like that other god of whom the ironical Tishbite spoke, he was talking, or he was pursuing, or he was in a journey, or he was sleeping and not to be awaked" (77; compare with 1 Kings 18:27). The observing narrator, the spiritual eye, is less concerned with motive or feeling than with pure spectacle, less indignant than visually attracted:

> The obscurity was now so great that [Alec] could see absolutely nothing but a pale nebulousness at his feet, which represented the white muslin figure he had left upon the dead leaves. Everything else was blackness alike. D'Urberville stooped; and heard a gentle regular breathing. He knelt, and bent lower, till her breath warmed his face, and in a moment his cheek was in contact with hers. She was sleeping soundly, and upon her eyelashes there lingered tears.
>
> Darkness and silence ruled everywhere around. Above them rose the primeval yews and oaks of The Chase, in which were poised gentle roosting birds in their last nap; and about them stole the hopping rabbits and hares. (76–77)

Hardy uses neither narrator to tell precisely what occurred. One wonders: Were there no words between Alec and Tess? Did she not awaken? Was there no struggle? All is left to inference; readers must "write" their own account of Alec's violation of Tess. Hardy refrains from telling us what actually occurred because public taste forbade describing a man raping a woman. Hardy dared not write a counterpart to the detached narrator's brutal sentence that vivifies the goring of the Durbeyfield horse: "The pointed shaft of the cart had entered the breast of the unhappy Prince like a sword; and from the wound his life's blood was spouting in a stream, and falling with a hiss into the road." Nor could he write a counterpart to this sentence: "In her despair Tess sprang forward and put her hand upon the hole, with the only result that she became helplessly splashed from face to skirt with . . . crimson drops." Instead of telling of a goring and Tess's response to a goring Hardy asks (in the guise of his narrator as moralist) about a coarse tracing and the injustice thereof: "Why it was that upon this beautiful feminine tissue, sensitive as gossamer, and practically blank as snow as yet, there should have been traced such a coarse pattern as it was doomed to receive; why so often the coarse appropriates the finer thus, the wrong man the woman, the wrong woman the man, many thousand years of analytical philosophy have failed to explain to our sense of order" (77).

By following Hardy's silent invitation to juxtapose, perhaps to superimpose, the mail cart's goring of Prince with Alec's tracing upon Tess, to marry events usually not intimate, the reader can perceive the beaugly: the wounding becomes a sexual assault; the accidental death of a horse becomes the premeditated brutalization of a human spirit. But what is the result? For how can we associate beauty with sexual violation? The connection is repugnant, obscene, cruel, the consequence of Hardy's restless imprisonment in language that serves a culture that oppresses women, and in at least two ways: through its silence about, its lacking words to describe women's experiences of sexual assault; and in its casualness in finding beauty in sexual violence against Tess and, at the same time, deploring that violence. Hardy is not free to use language as candidly as he would like. But language, as the product in nineteenth-century England of a dominantly male culture, does not contain readily available words for a rape victim's experience of rape as goring. So Hardy creates that experience—for the imaginative reader—by inviting the reader to fuse the goring of a horse and the rape of a virgin. Hardy's divided narrative voice—a moralizer conversing, so to speak, with a detached observer about the agony of Tess—is evidence of a failure of sympathy.

Just as the reader gropes for words to describe as beautiful what registers as horrible, so also Hardy experiences a similar reaching after words. Not just Hardy's notorious revisions of this episode,[18] but also his rhetoric in his "final" version suggests his wish to create uncertainty about just how to tell of the event. This is most evident in his repeated use of questions to elicit from his reader an explanation for Tess's undoing: Where is her guardian angel? Where is the providence of her Christian faith? Why is one so sensitive as she the victim of such coarse trespass? Why, in general, does the coarse appropriate the fine? His answers to his own questions are tentative. Perhaps Tess's Christian providence is as weak as those pagan gods of the priests of Baal whom Elijah taunts in the Old Testament (1 Kings 18:27). Perhaps Tess's treatment is retribution for her powerful ancestors' assaults on peasant girls. Perhaps Tess's ruin is simply something that has to occur, something written in the book of fate, something predestined.

Hardy creates an air of inexplicability because to explain would be to destroy the beauty in ugliness of the event. To explain why rather than to ask why would also enclose the entire issue in the accepted philosophical and theological doctrines of his times. But Hardy's originality in *Tess* lies precisely in his refusal to adopt constraining norms, whether artistic or theological. His creative courage rests in his determination to diverge from what had come before. He chooses not to judge Tess and her violators, for then he would be simply telling a moral tale. He chooses instead to judge them and at the same time to record, free of moral consideration, the appearances of things around them. Hardy makes the rape of Tess an epiphany by the way in which he depicts the scene. The strikingness of the event shows a grasp on human reality—and that grasp on reality is what is original.

Hardy is certain (in the language of his moralizing narrator) that "an immeasurable social chasm was to divide . . . [Tess's] personality thereafter from that previous self of hers who stepped from her mother's door to try her fortune at Trantridge poultry-farm" (77). Just as after the death of Prince Tess finds she has become someone else, a stranger to herself, a "murderess," so, also, after Alec has plundered her innocence, she becomes a sinner (38). Several weeks after the violation, Hardy describes her as estranged from herself because she has learned to see terror in beauty. She is returning to "the familiar green world" (81) of her native Vale of Blakemore, conscious that she sees things differently. The "always beautiful" Vale has become "terribly beautiful to Tess to-day" because since last seeing it she has learned "that the serpent hisses where the sweet birds sing" (81). This discovery that serpent and bird, hiss and warble, terror and pleasure coexist has "totally changed" her views of life (81). Neither Tess nor the reader can know why she was violated; what she, and we, can know is the effect of that violation: Tess gains the ability to perceive beauty in "the deeper reality underlying the scenic"; she awakens to "the [beauty in the] tragical mysteries of life" (*Life,* 185). In this deeper seeing and awakening the beauty of her rape/goring presumably lies.

But this terrible beauty has another effect on Tess: it arouses in her a lethal hatred and anger, which she displays almost immediately as she trudges on toward her home in Blakemore Vale after having spent a few weeks with Alec. Alec appears behind her, rebuking her for sneaking out of his house and showing little sympathy for his feelings. When she tells him she never expected he would rape her, he makes what will prove to be a fatal error by telling her, in effect, that she is like all other women: she invites and welcomes sexual subjugation. Her explosive response proves that his violation of her has made her capable of violence, the first such instance Hardy has depicted in her. Whereas at the death of Prince she can blame only herself, here she can rightly blame Alec: "'How can you dare to use such words!' she cried, turning impetuously upon him, her eyes flashing as the latent spirit (of which he was to see more some day) awoke in her. 'My God, I could knock you out of the gig! Did it ever strike your mind that what every woman says some women may feel?'" (83).

Tess's refusal of Alec's offer to provide for her as his mistress reveals a "scorn" untypical of her "large and impulsive nature" (83). Tess has, indeed, become "another girl than the simple one she had been at home" (81). Without so much as a blush, she stands "like a marble term" and accepts Alec's farewell kiss. Immediately thereafter, she brings down similar scornful anger on the head of a man who prints punitive biblical texts—in bright red paint—on barns and gates throughout the countryside. The offensive spiritual inscribings of this Christian author remind Tess and the reader of Alec's "inscription" on her in The Chase. The preacher's lurid writings, Alec's forced inscription, Prince's goring—all involve trespass. The death of a horse, the violation of a woman, the perversion of religious teaching—in this fusion of disparates is beaugliness. Tess watches as the fanatical preacher inscribes a text and gores a precious doctrine:

> He . . . began painting large square letters on the middle board of the three composing the stile; placing a comma after each word, as if to give pause while that word was driven well home to the reader's heart,
>
> THY, DAMNATION, SLUMBERETH, NOT.
> 2 PET. ii. 3.

The Goring of Tess

Against the peaceful landscape, the pale decaying tints of the copses, the blue air of the horizon, and the lichened stile-boards, these staring vermillion words shone forth. They seemed to shout themselves out, and make the atmosphere ring. Some people might have cried 'Alas, poor Theology!' at the hideous defacement—the last grotesque phase of a creed which had served mankind well in its time. But the words entered Tess with accusatory horror: it was as if this man had known her recent history; yet he was a total stranger. (85)

The repetitions among the three episodes—the goring, the rape, the words of the transcriptions that "entered Tess"—are less interesting than the question Hardy, in varied ways, asks through them: Whence comes the beauty in these violations, in these trespassings? To offer an answer is less important than to note that Hardy is insistently asking the question, skillfully figuring and refiguring its asking, in developing his two major characters—Tess and Angel—as well as in employing his divided narrative.

Hardy repeats the question, but this time "monumentally" when, he sets Tess's helpless rage upon being importuned yet again by Alec in an eerie spot named Cross-in-Hand (see illustration opposite beginning of chapter 4): "Of all spots on the bleached and desolate upland this was the most forlorn. It was so far removed from the charm which is sought in landscape by artists and view-lovers as to reach a new kind of beauty, a negative beauty of tragic tone" (302). Hardy provides several explanations for the origin and meaning of this virtual monument to a new kind of beauty. First, his observing narrator, speaking here as a historian, reports that the stone was not of local origin and that a human hand had been carved on it. Some authorities, this learned narrator explains, believe it is the relic of a devotional cross; some believe it is simply a boundary marker. Alec, a recent convert to Christianity, also believes that the pillar was once a holy cross and asks that Tess put her hand on it and swear never again to tempt him. But a shepherd, untutored and unconverted, provides Tess with yet another account, an "unexpectedly gruesome" (302) one that frightens her: far from being the remnant of a holy cross, the monument is what remains of a stone post erected by relatives of a criminal, a man who made a bargain with Satan, a man the authorities tortured by nailing his hand to the post then hanged and buried on the spot. By this particular account Cross-in-Hand resembles the novel *Tess*: both monument and novel are memorials to executed malefactors.

Hardy associates the new beauty of this spot, the new beauty of *Tess,* not with something known or even knowable, but rather with Cross-in-Hand's mysterious embodiment of contraries: Is it a cross or gallows? Is it a monument to Christ or to Satan? Was it the scene of the torture and execution of a criminal or the site of the death of a martyr? At Cross-in-Hand we hear the serpent hissing where the sweet birds sing. Hardy's phrase "negative beauty of tragic tone" merely hints at an explanation: the paradoxical beauty resides in the ugliness of the violence of execution, in the darker doings of humankind, doings whose results cannot be undone. One might suggest then that this negative beauty resides in the sad truth that all things move deathward, irretrievably deathward. As suggested earlier, Hardy's recurrent interest in beauty in ugliness is less a theme than a refrain, less an argument than a lyric, a recurring chorus to which he contributes the colors of the words, events, and settings.

We know Tess's dream of happiness in love, and it is enough, perhaps, to know that she dreamed and will die without fulfilling that dream; we know she dies bewildered by excess of love; we know she changes utterly, and that with her change an ugly beauty, a beauty fed by her agonies, is born. Explanation is less important than transforming death and death's inevitability into something that nourishes life, that is, something that stirs human consciousness to the depth of its capacity to contemplate enduring. What could stir more deeply than transforming loss into gain, however chastened the gain may be?

9

A Face Like the Sun's

Thus far we have noted that in the death of a horse on the road to Casterbridge, in the execution of Tess at Wintoncester, in Alec's violation of Tess in The Chase, Hardy has depicted Tess's beaugliness as a quality of the victim. In chapter 14, however, Hardy shows us the beaugliness in Tess's new role as aggressor and violator, for she defies the marginal status assigned to the fieldwomen and makes herself into a man-woman whose power rivals the supremacy of both men and the "male" sun god. She shows her new defiance in several ways: in the love-hate she shows for her infant son as she suckles and then violently kisses him; in the transformation she effects in herself, her family, and her surroundings in order to baptize her son when her father has forbade the parson to carry out the baptism; in her determination to see that her dead infant is properly buried, because the parson will not allow burial in consecrated ground.

Hardy depicts the growing beaugliness of Tess's role as aggressor/violator by noting its effects on her face: pointing to the "immaculate beauty" and "glowing irradiation" of her face as she presides at the baptism; the contemptuous affection on her face as she suckles and violently kisses her infant son; her multishaded bottomless eyes that even an enemy would soften before; and her "eye of maternal affection" and its vision of love and devotion as she buries her dead child.

As an evocation of beauty in ugliness, chapter 14 of *Tess* is an astonishing tour de force, an evocation of the beaugly startling even in a novel sharply accented by such moments, and an evocation especially noteworthy because Hardy locates the beaugly in faces—faces of men, women, and children, the faces of the sun and the moon, but most particularly in the face of Tess Durbeyfield.

Soon after Tess returns to her native Marlott she gives birth to a son, whom she belatedly names Sorrow. She withstands the at times harsh curiosity of friends and neighbors, and then—in a resurgence of spirit—joins in the hard work of the harvest; for the corn is ripe in the fields around Marlott and every able hand is needed to bring it in: "After wearing and wasting her palpitating heart with every engine of regret that lonely inexperience could devise, common-sense had illumined her. She felt that she would do well to be useful again—to taste anew sweet independence at any price. The past was past; whatever it had been it was no more at hand" (96).

Hardy's creation of the beaugly here begins with this surge of hope in Tess (Hardy views it as an "illumination"), a hope he dramatizes by placing it within the entire chapter's strongly rhythmic, even choreographic, movements. Hardy's harvest scene—a much favored subject of nineteenth-century artists—is emphatically rhythmical: his reaping machine moves round and round the fields with the regularity of the rising and setting of the sun; his fieldwomen, Tess among them, move "like dancers in a quadrille" (94) as they gather the sheaves; and Tess's child dances the most elemental of all dances by moving from birth through briefest life to death.

The first of the faces to emerge among these interlocking movements is that of the morning sun, whose warm beams penetrate and dissolve the vapors of night and whose gender Hardy makes, somewhat curiously, explicitly masculine: "The sun, on account of the mist, had a curious, sentient, personal look, demanding the masculine pronoun for its adequate expression.... His light a little later broke through chinks of cottage shutters, throwing stripes like red-hot pokers upon cupboards, chests of drawers, and other furniture within; and awakening harvesters who were not already astir" (92). Why, one wonders, is this warming, wakening agent also a violent intruder? And why, one most wonders, does the "curious, sentient, personal look" on the face of this August morning sun require "the masculine pronoun for its adequate expression"? Are the faces of women, and are women themselves, as the text implies, without curiosity, sentience, and personality? Is the pronoun "she" somehow inadequate to express this luminary's "beaming, mild-eyed" godlikeness? Why is this father- or brother-sun, rather than sister- or mother-sun? We will attempt to answer these questions later, and note then their connections with Hardy's combining of beauty and ugliness in the face of Tess, a face that in the course of the chapter comes to rival in its beaugliness the face of the beamingly beautiful masculine sun.

It is worth noting here that Hardy persists in the odd suggestion that men enjoy a personality denied women; for just a few sentences later, after the observing narrator describes the reapers' slaughter of rabbits, hares, snakes, rats, and mice, Hardy takes pains to distinguish between fieldmen and fieldwomen, describing the latter as the more interesting: "by reason of the charm . . . acquired by woman when she becomes part and parcel of outdoor nature, and [she] is not merely an object set down therein as at ordinary times. A field-man is a personality afield; a field-woman is a portion of the field; she has somehow lost her own margin, imbibed the essence of her surrounding, and assimilated herself with it" (93).

The face of the morning sun, because it is personal, has to be masculine; a fieldman is a personality when in the field, but a field-woman is an impersonal, if more charming, segment of the field. Yet this is not the case with Tess. Unlike her sisters among the work-women, she retains her own margin, even trespasses upon the margins of others, particularly the men around her. For amongst these impersonal and charming field segments, amongst these marginless and yet appealing female persons, Tess is at first faceless, but only for the moment; because she has pulled her bonnet "so far over her brow that none of her face is disclosed" (93). But she will free her face from the

shadow of her bonnet—that venerable symbol of female reticence—
and thrust it forward to rival the sun's, as well as the faces of the other
males that look on her. Hardy's unveiling of Tess's beaugliful face in
the course of this chapter—in counterpoint to the glowingly beautiful
masculine face of the sun, and to the glowering masculine faces of
John Durbeyfield and the village clergyman—focuses his effort to
work yet another variation on the beaugly. The emergence of Tess's
face is the emergence of beaugliness in the form unique to her, a breaking through of a quality of person, and personality, that is not mere
charm and not simply hope breaking through the shadows cast over
her face by her memory of rape, or by shame, self-contempt, gossip,
and parental and clerical obtuseness.

The emergence of Tess's beautiful-ugly face is the emergence of
the face of a dancer from the dance, the emergence of an individual
personality from the impersonality of process, pattern, and social pre-
scription. Imagine a dance troupe moving concertedly, predictably,
and in unison across a stage; then one member of that troupe steps
away from the rest, breaking the pattern and moving toward the on-
lookers, slowing lifting her head to expose her face as she advances to
center stage to become the focus of attention: this suggests Hardy's
way of governing the movement of the chapter and gradually separat-
ing Tess from fieldwomen, fieldmen, and the sun, so that he can finally
reveal her resplendent beaugliness.

First we see emerging from beneath the bonnet "the oval face of
a handsome young woman with deep dark eyes and long heavy cling-
ing tresses, . . . [with] . . . cheeks . . . paler, . . . teeth more regular,
[and] . . . red lips thinner than is usual in a country-bred girl" (94).
Tess's movements as she works are likened to a dance that radiates the
beaugly:

> Her binding proceeds with clock-like monotony. From the sheaf last
> finished she draws a handful of ears, patting their tips with her left
> palm to bring them even. Then stooping low she moves forward,
> gathering the corn with both hands against her knees, and pushing
> her left gloved hand under the bundle to meet the right on the other
> side, holding the corn in an embrace like that of a lover. She brings

the ends of the bond together, and kneels on the sheaf while she ties it, beating back her skirts now and then when lifted by the breeze. A bit of her naked arm is visible between the buff leather of the gauntlet and the sleeve of her gown; and as the day wears on its feminine smoothness becomes scarified by the stubble, and bleeds. (94)

Tess binding the sheaves is machinelike but also something else—she is passionately loving in her "holding the corn in an embrace like that of a lover," modest in her concern lest the breeze raise her skirts, vulnerable in that she bleeds when the stubble chafes her tender skin. The "feminine smoothness . . . scarified" and bloodied by the wheat ends recalls in graphic terms Alec's tracing a coarse pattern on her "beautiful feminine tissue" (77).

The commingling of beauty and ugliness on Tess's face may be a result of Tess's having to accept contradictions within her life. One such contradiction is Tess's unprotesting participation in the slaughter of creatures ensnared by the encircling, centripetal, dancelike progress of the harvesters.

As noted, the movements of the harvesters are rhythmic and regular, dancelike in their progress. Two groups, one male the other female, enter the field; the harvesting machine, its "ticking like the love-making of a grasshopper" (92), circles the field from its margins toward its center, reducing the standing grain to a smaller and smaller area as the morning wears on—all this under the beaming eyes of the warm (and masculine) August sun. Under this luminous masculine face, the wild creatures of the field—rodents and serpents—"retreated inwards as into a fastness, unaware of the ephemeral nature of their refuge, and of the doom that awaited them later in the day when, their covert shrinking to a more and more horrible narrowness, they were huddled together friends and foes, till the last few yards of upright wheat fell also under the teeth of the unerring reaper, and they were every one put to death by the sticks and stones of the harvesters" (93). Although this bloodbath is emblematic of Tess's victimization, Hardy does not exclude Tess from the ranks of the executioners/harvesters, and he does not even hint that this slaughter in which his otherwise tenderhearted heroine joins somehow mars the scenic appeal of the symmetry and ritual of the harvest in the warm August sunshine. This scene, much celebrated for its descriptive beauty by readers of Hardy from the 1890s to the present, glorifies communal work and communal slaughter. This is clearly not a harvest scene typical of nineteenth-century pastoral art because these field-workers are grim reapers as well as reapers of grain, agents of death as well as producers of the staff of life.

If readers have not frequently registered the cruelty of Tess and these slaughterers, it is perhaps because readers tacitly edit as they read, silently divesting Tess of responsibility. Perhaps readers view the slaughter of the animals as a version of the coming slaughter of Tess and conclude that the entire cruel episode is Hardy's attempt to underline the cruelty in society's treatment of Tess. The beauty in ugliness, ugliness in beauty, which accompanies Tess like her shadow, lies in the irony of the victim who plays not just the victimizer, but the executioner, that is, the legitimized, community-sanctioned killer. There is irony in Tess's lovely and pitiful face being an unknowingly cruel face. The irony lies in the masked, Janusian reality that hosts the beaugly, that is, the beautiful and the uncategorized, unrationalized, unponderable ugliness of reality.

There is nothing new, of course, in the idea that farm work, the work of planting and gathering, requires brutal killing, but Hardy's way of showing a beauty in its logic is new and unsettling. For by insisting that there is ugliness in beauty he is refusing to allow the moral horror in that beauty's logic to overbalance the beautiful, insisting that to see and to learn to admire the beauty in the horrid illogic of things is to pluck a good out of evil. Hardy has found a way to justify the ways of the gods to men and women, and the ways of men and women to other men and women, and to other living creatures.

Unwilling to declare there is no beauty, no source of pleasure for common men and women, Hardy retains the concept of beauty in a new form, because the conditions of modern life exact new understanding of what is beautiful. To insist that the beautiful is that which pleases according to traditional standards is, in Hardy's view, to succumb to the inevitable selectiveness of such standards, selectiveness that often serves the needs of the privileged and empowered groups who shape, promulgate, and enforce such norms.

A second instance of the beaugly is the episode—easily regarded as merely a bit of naturalistic detail—in which Tess interrupts her work to suckle her infant. Her siblings bring to her "what at first sight seemed to be a doll, but proved to be an infant in long clothes" (94–95). Tess sits it upright in her lap, then looks away from it "with a gloomy indifference that was almost dislike," then, suddenly and violently crushing her face against its, "fell to . . . kissing it some dozens of times, as if she could never leave off, the child crying at the vehemence of an onset which strangely combined passionateness with contempt" (95).

Tess's fellow laborers discern her love-hate feelings toward her child, and in shaping their observations Hardy uses humor, of all things, to turn the pain in this desperate face to face encounter of mother and son into something less painful, to expose through laughter another version of the beaugly:

> 'She's fond of that there child, though she mid pretend to hate en, and say she wishes the baby and her too were in the church-yard', observed the woman in the red petticoat.
>
> 'She'll soon leave off saying that,' replied the one in buff. 'Lord, 'tis wonderful what a body can get used to o' that sort in time!'
>
> 'A little more than persuading had to do wi' the coming o't, I reckon. There were they that heard a sobbing one night last year in The Chase; and it mid ha' gone hard wi' a certain party if folks had come along.'
>
> 'Well, a little more, or a little less, 'twas a thousand pities that it should have happened to she, of all others—hey, Jenny?' The speaker turned to one of the group who certainly was not ill-defined as plain. (95)

With humor's irreverence for familiar forms and feelings Hardy can thrust aside the mere compassion of the first speaker, the threadbare realism of the second, and the futile indignation of the third in favor of a feeling less familiar, and less tender. He exacts of his reader a bittersweet (and nastily male) laughter; bitter because it is at the expense of homely Jenny, but sweet because the joke brings beauty to Tess Durbeyfield's suffering. Hardy invokes the beaugly by matching Tess with her opposite, by joining a woman whose ugly face protects her virtue with a woman whose beautiful face constantly jeopardizes hers.

One recalls the cruel conversation between Tess's parents upon her departure from Marlott in Alec's cart:

> [Joan:] 'Well, as one of the genuine stock, she ought to make her way with 'en, if she plays her trump card aright. And if he don't marry her afore he will after. For that he's all afire wi' love for her any eye can see.'
> [John:] 'What's her trump card? Her d'Urberville blood, you mean?'
> [Joan:] 'No, stupid; her face—as 'twas mine.' (55)

As the women discuss Tess her face burns with rising color, and we see "her flower-like mouth and large tender eyes, neither black nor blue nor grey nor violet; rather all these shades together, and a hundred others, which could be seen if one looked into their irises—shade behind shade—tint beyond tint—around pupils that had no bottom" (95–96). The redness of the blush dispelled by the black-blue-grey-violet of her eyes is a chromatic stroke of beaugliness, its origins and nature behind and beyond color, unfathomable because they combine then recombine and are finally beyond the range of colors to which the human eye can respond.

Tess's beautiful face, her potential material salvation, is the source of her ruin. In this chapter a Janus-faced creature emerges, a Tess-Jenny, a beautiful-ugly faced creature, a woman with two faces. We saw earlier that upon leaving Marlott for work elsewhere Tess mutilates her face, makes herself ugly, makes herself a Jenny so that she will not attract the attention of men. But one must note here the additional pain—call it the Jenny-pain—this humor requires that one contemplate along with Tess's pain.

This illusion of relief, mingling laughter with tears, a virtuous-ugly Jenny-face with a ruined-beautiful Tess-face, is here the basis for the beaugly. Hardy repeats it, only a few paragraphs later, when his moral narrator observes the odd acceptance Tess has gained from the other reapers as they leave the field for their homes at sunset:

> Tess's female companions sang songs, and showed themselves very sympathetic and glad at her reappearance out of doors, though they could not refrain from mischievously throwing in a few verses of the ballad about the maid who went to the merry green wood and came back in a changed state. There are counterpoises and compensations in life; and the event which had made of her a social warning had also for the moment made her the most interesting personage in the village to many. Their friendliness won her still further away from herself, their lively spirits were contagious, and she became almost gay. (97)

"[A]lmost gay"—the mischievous friendliness of Tess's companions produces *in* her a near happiness that corresponds precisely to the near beauty that makes her "the most interesting personage in the village to many" at the same time that she is to them "a social warning."

Hardy's most dramatic creation of the beaugly in chapter 14 is his account of Tess's baptism of her dying child. When Hardy published the serial version of *Tess*, he was forced to exclude this episode—as well as the chapters in which he depicted Alec's violation of Tess—because the editor of the *Graphic* found it objectionable. Ever resourceful, Hardy published chapter 14 separately, as a short story of sorts, in another magazine, the *Fortnightly Review,* under the title "The Midnight Baptism, A Study in Christianity." So chapter 14 appeared in print two months before the serial of *Tess* was published, from July to December 1891, but when he published *Tess* in volume form in November of the same year, he had reinstated the chapter to the text.

It is worth pondering that Hardy's editor viewed Alec's violation of the virginal Tess and Tess's baptism of her dying son as somehow comparably offensive on moral grounds. As we have seen in the previous chapter, Tess's violation by Alec, given its disturbing echoes of the goring of Tess's horse, is an extreme instance of the beaugly. Apart from finding it offensive because it is a scene (however inexplicit) of sexual violation, the editor of the *Graphic* no doubt found it difficult to discern Hardy's attitude toward the event, given the contending views of his observing and moralizing narrators, one recording the beauties of the event, the other lamenting its injustice. The editor must have found similarly ambivalent, and no doubt somewhat sacrilegious, Hardy's attitude toward the Anglican clergy and the sacred rite of baptism, especially since Tess recites a good deal of the actual language for the ministration of that sacrament from the Anglican Book of Common Prayer.

Once she knows her son will soon die, Tess eagerly seeks his baptism because, ironically, she wants for him precisely what Angel wants for her—purity: "Tess had drifted into a frame of mind which accepted passively consideration that, if she should have to burn for what she had done, burn she must, and there was an end of it. . . . But when the same question arose with regard to the baby, it had a different colour. Her darling was about to die, and no salvation" (97). But her drunken father, still sensitive to the supposed smudge the child's illegitimacy has set upon his decrepit family name, refuses to allow the village parson to enter his cottage to administer the sacrament. Tess, instinctively orthodox in such matters, fears that if her child dies unbaptized it will be "consigned to the nethermost corner of hell as its double doom for lack of baptism and lack of legitimacy" (98). Murmuring incoherent and desperate prayers, she suddenly decides to baptize the infant herself: "Ah, perhaps baby can be saved! Perhaps it will be just the same!" (98).

Hardy's comment on this exclamation—he uses the idiom of his aesthetic narrator—plucks Tess's face out of the darkness of her bedroom and out of her despair in a puzzling way: "She spoke so brightly that it seems as though her face might have shone in the gloom surrounding her" (98). What does it mean to speak "brightly"? Does it mean hopefully? cheerfully? The shift from declarative to subjunctive mood—from "she spoke" to "it seems as though her face might have shone"—in the space of this short sentence is intriguing because it reveals Hardy contemplating the possibility of the beaugly in Tess's face rather than describing its presence. Hardy extracts the beaugly grammatically, from the space between what happens and what appears to be happening. Tess's face mirrors her hope at the same time that it is a window into her despair. Her face reflects as it illuminates and is a mirror at the same time that it is a lamp. Her face is not just a beautiful object; it is a shifting, changing indicator of Tess's state of being.

The brightness of her face begins to rival that of the masculine sun, whose powerful beams melt nights and mists to bring on mornings and to regulate the lives of all creatures on the earth. Tess's solar powers are real, for she transforms a dark and desperate occasion into a bright and hopeful one by willing the transformation of herself and her surroundings, and this transformation—because it mingles the holy and the profane—is her production and direction of the beaugly. She does this, not with the power of borrowed or reflected light as the moon might, but—like the sun—with powers inherent in her.

Her achievement is a wonderful effort of make-believe. She first wakens her brothers and sisters and requires that they kneel with folded hands, as if they were members of a congregation witnessing a baptism. Or perhaps she sees these sleepy children as filling the role of the godmothers and godfathers required by the words of the rite in the prayer book, which Liza-Lu holds open before Tess. The decrepit Durbeyfield cottage is itself transformed by Tess's brightness; for it becomes her make-believe church, and the cottage's homely washstand and water jug in the children's bedroom become her baptismal stand and font. One of the Durbeyfield daughters becomes "the clerk at church" (98), holding open the prayer book before another daughter—the one who had brought disgrace to the family by conceiving a child out of wedlock.

What is more, this mother of a bastard and daughter of a drunk and a slattern, this "woman . . . [of] slight incautiousness of character inherited from her race" (96), ordains herself a man of the cloth, a parson, an adult male invested—by herself and not by a bishop—with the power to baptize. The purity she cannot offer Angel she confers on her son. Baptism is, of course, a sacred rite in which a priest (until very recently always male) purifies an infant of original sin and thereby confers on the newborn spiritual rebirth and membership in the community of believers. In assuming a role traditionally and prescriptively held by a man, this woman-man has come to rival the emphatically male morning sun.

No doubt the conservative editor of the *Graphic* feared most the response of genteel readers to Hardy's weird mingling of piety and heterodoxy—his creation of an aesthetically and theologically unorthodox beauty—in the sentences in which Tess mimes the Book of Common Prayer. More so than today, a great number of Hardy's readers in the 1890s would have been conversant enough with the language of the Book of Common Prayer to respond indignantly to the impieties in Tess's pastoral efforts.

After borrowing the name Sorrow from Genesis to name her dying child, Tess, with only slight alterations, speaks the language of the prayer book as she sprinkles the child with water:

> 'SORROW, I baptize thee in the name of the Father, and of the Son, and of the Holy Ghost.' . . .
> Tess went on: 'We receive this child'—and so forth—'and do sign him with the sign of the cross.' Here she dipped her hand into the basin, and fervently drew an immense cross upon the baby with her forefinger; continuing with the customary sentences as to his manfully fighting against sin, the world, and the devil; and being a faithful soldier and servant unto his life's end. . . . She duly went on with the Lord's Prayer, the children lisping it after her in a thin, gnat-like wail; till at the conclusion, raising their voices to clerk's pitch, they again piped into the silence, 'A---men!'. (99)

Then, "with much augmented confidence in the efficacy of this sacrament," Tess "boldly and triumphantly" recites the thanksgiving that follows, a prayer Hardy omits entirely. But if Hardy omitted the actual words of the thanksgiving, he wrote lavishly of the sound of that prayer pouring from Tess's mouth and describes that feature of Tess's face to which he refers most frequently throughout the novel:

A Face Like the Sun's

[She reads] in the stopt-diapason note which her voice acquired
when her heart was in her speech, and which will never be forgotten
by those who knew her. The ecstasy of faith almost apotheosized
her; it set upon her face a glowing irradiation and brought a red
spot into the middle of each cheek; while the miniature candle-
flame inverted in her eye-pupils shone like a diamond. The children
gazed up at her with more and more reverence, and no longer had
a will for questioning. She did not look like Sissy to them now, but
as a being large, towering and awful, a divine personage with whom
they had nothing in common. (99–100)

By depicting her transforming her cottage, its furnishings, and occu-
pants into a church and its parishioners; transforming her dying infant
son from one damned to one saved; transforming herself from unwed
mother into minister and priest—all out of desperate faith in her own
powers and love for her child—Hardy proposes that her creative force
rivals that of the male sun. Tess's strange beauty, particularly her
strange beauty of countenance, flourishes in the midst of otherwise
ugly surroundings and events because Hardy refuses to subject her to
moral judgment, refuses to hold her to conventional codes that would
call her mad, sinful, impious, pathetic, unfortunate, or ignorant. He
makes the same refusal even earlier, at the onset of the ceremony: "Her
figure looked singularly tall and imposing as she stood in her long
white night-gown. . . . The kindly dimness of the weak candle ab-
stracted from her form and features the little blemishes which sunlight
might have revealed—the stubble scratches upon her wrists, and the
weariness of her eyes—her high enthusiasm having a transfiguring effect upon the face which had been her undoing, showing it as a thing
of immaculate beauty, with a touch of dignity which was almost regal"
(99).

Hardy's language in the three episodes we have discussed suggests
that he has indeed raised up Tess—as "divine personage" with a face
of "immaculate beauty" and a "dignity . . . almost regal"—to rival the
masculine sun that shines down upon the villagers of Marlott. No
small part of her power, her capacity to violate received practices and
values, is her assuming the traditionally male role of priest of the An-

glican faith, an act whose legitimacy she confirms when she confronts the village parson about Christian burial for Sorrow the Undesired. Although the parson agrees, against his better judgment, that Tess's "extemporized ordinance" will be just the same as if he had baptized Sorrow himself (100), he refuses Sorrow a Christian burial. But then, responding to "the dignity of the girl, [and] the strange tenderness in her voice" (100), he assures her that burying the child in unhallowed ground will be just the same as burying him in sacred earth. When Tess is forced to bury the body of her child among the bodies of the unholy, Hardy evokes his most wrenching instance of the beaugly:

> [T]he baby was carried in a small deal box, under an ancient woman's shawl, to the churchyard that night, and buried by lantern-light, at the cost of a shilling and a pint of beer to the sexton, in that shabby corner of God's allotment where He lets the nettles grow, and where all unbaptized infants, notorious drunkards, suicides, and others of the conjecturally damned are laid. In spite of the untoward surroundings, however, Tess bravely made a little cross of two laths and a piece of string, and having bound it with flowers, she stuck it up at the head of the grave one evening when she could enter the churchyard without being seen, putting at the foot also a bunch of the same flowers in a little jar of water to keep them alive. What matter was it that on the outside of the jar the eye of mere observation noted the words 'Keelwell's Marmalade'? The eye of maternal affection did not see them in its vision of higher things. (101)

The detached narrator speaks in the first two sentences, and then the narrative breaks, so to speak, to the voice of his moral commentator, the speaker of the last two sentences. Tess here extemporizes the ordinance for the burial of the dead just as she had the order for baptism of the dying. And now, as then, she transforms the occasion, then with her version of the language of the sacred rite, here with her love for her dead child. Against the damned, she sets the infant she has saved; against the nettles she sets a wooden cross bound with flowers; against "the eye of mere observation" she sets the "eye of maternal affection" and its "vision of higher things," by which Hardy can only mean a love that transcends even the divine love represented by the Vicar of Marlott, that pathetic product of "ten years of endeavour to graft technical belief on actual scepticism" (100). In her sheer faith, this ruined mother of Sorrow is more priest than the man of the cloth.

Tess transforms herself, and her surroundings, through the depth of her love because for her belief and practice are of a piece. Consequently, one sees beauty in her commonplaceness and the commonplaceness of her surroundings: a "vision of higher things" in a "Keelwell's Marmalade" jar; the cross of Christ in "a little cross of two laths and a piece of string"; an infant purified of original sin buried among the "conjecturally damned"; a seemingly ordinary woman displaying extraordinary powers, including those traditionally invested in men both secular and divine.

In chapter 14 Hardy illustrates that his sense of the beaugly is deeply rooted in his hatred of privilege and prescriptive social and political inequity. The emphatically masculine and godlike morning sun that "breaks through chinks of cottage shutters, throwing stripes like red-hot pokers upon cupboards, chests of drawers, and other furniture within" (92) recalls unmistakably the wealthy Alec's sexual trespass upon his peasant cousin, an act she will reciprocate when she—returning violence for violence—stabs him to death. But even before that retribution, Tess rehearses as it were her revenge on the male figures who torment her: the father who blocks the baptism of her child, the parson who refuses to sanctify the child's burial, the masculine sun that beams down on her misery. Tess fights back by enacting the roles of superior humanity herself, assuming the authority for which neither her father nor the parson is equipped, attaining a depth of feeling that approaches a higher vision, but one of her own making. By chapter's end, a radiance in Tess's baptism and burial of her bastard son by candlelight and lantern light has come to rival and surpass the radiance of the sun at morning because beauty of will, love, and courage shines through, without displacing, the ugliness of despair, fear, and near madness that drives her to act as she does. Hardy depicts the beaugly in Tess's ultimately futile refusal to be just another marginless girl of her village, her refusal to contemplate her son's burial without baptism, her determination that in death her son will be treated differently than the rest of the unsanctified bodies buried in the pauper's corner of the Marlott cemetary.

Hardy's notion of the beaugly, even in the context of this strongly antireligious chapter, has a distinctly spiritual flavor and reflects anything but the pessimism frequently attributed to him. The seer of beauty in ugliness is, for Hardy, one who sees in the phenomena of human time and circumstances qualities in themselves resplendent that do not point toward something higher, deeper, or greater than themselves. Hardy's repeated invocation of the beaugly in and around Tess is a stubborn insistence on the sufficiency of things mortal, mundane, and ordinary to satisfy the loudest cries of the human spirit.

10

Rally as Defeat

Hardy titled the third phase of Tess's career "The Rally," and by this he means "the recovery," although given the strength of his notion that her tragedy is irreparable, it is unlikely that Tess will ever recover. As we know, Tess ends far worse than she begins, as a convicted murderer executed under the strictest terms of the law; the close of her life is not unlike that of the malefactor who is memorialized at Cross-in-Hand.

Hardy is using his metaphor for recovery ironically: to denote a rally that is not a rally. Tess's rally is really a defeat, a resounding defeat at that, because in gaining hope, happiness, and love, in forgetting human imperfection and fate, she sets herself up for her tragic defeat. Hardy reminds us of such imperfection and fate and points to the folly of Tess's idealized love by evoking the beaugliness surrounding Tess's happiness through the upending of conventional imagery.

Recovering her vital powers is precisely the effect, at least initially, of Tess's decision to leave her native Marlott to find work at Talbothays Dairy after she has buried her child. The season of her departure is the spring, and it would seem that Tess has regained a full zest for life, that she is indeed rallying from her defeats. Her destination, the

Valley of the Great Dairies, is a cheering and nurturing place. Talbot-hays Dairy is a flourishing farm; the dairyman, his wife, and his workers are a community of willing labor; the land is lush and bountiful. Although Tess's spirits soar—she hears "a pleasant voice in every breeze" (109)—her face, somewhat ominously, suggests that not all is well. The detached narrator describes the shifting beauty of Tess's face, a visage capable of combining, as we have seen, human misery and divine transcendence: "Her face . . . changed with changing states of mind, continually fluctuating between beauty and ordinariness, according as the thoughts were gay or grave. One day she was pink and flawless; another pale and tragical. When she was pink she was feeling less than when pale; her more perfect beauty accorded with her less elevated mood; her more intense mood with her less perfect beauty" (109).

Here Hardy establishes a ratio between beauty and, not ugliness, but "ordinariness." Although one would expect precisely the opposite—that beauty would accompany gaiety rather than gravity of thought—Tess's beauty is not, as we know, conventional beauty: hers is the beauty of ordinariness and the beauty of tragic experience. Since the encounter with Alec and the death of her child Tess has changed from a simple girl into a complex woman who is capable of violence. The interchange of beauties, pink and pale, gay and grave, in her articulate face suggests her new complexity.

When Hardy stages the enigmatic meeting of Tess and Clare in the unkempt garden of the dairy, he is also seeking to dramatize the difference in Tess that will allow her to be capable of stalking a man, being the aggressor rather than the victim who is trespassed against.

Tess is in this state of what one might call "inverse beauty" when she meets Angel Clare (for the second time, she recalls), the man whose love she somehow knows can help her effect full recovery. They converge, rather than merely fall in love, moving toward one another as if driven by the same forces that move the waters of the many streams of the lush Valley of the Great Dairies into one another and toward the sea.

Tess is wandering alone in the weedy garden when she hears the sound of Angel playing a harp. If Hardy's best efforts on behalf of beaugliness in earlier scenes were visual and tactile, his best efforts here are tactile and auditory. The impression he seeks is somewhat familiar by now, a commingling of the pleasing with, in this particular case, the sensuously disgusting.

In this scene Tess is again captivated by her surroundings and falls into a semiconscious trance. First she hears the "strumming of strings": "Dim flattened, constrained by their confinement, they had never appealed to her as now, when they wandered in the still air with a stark quality like that of nudity. . . . [As] she listened Tess, like a fascinated bird, could not leave the spot. Far from leaving she drew up towards the performer, keeping behind the hedge that he might not guess her presence" (127). Next Hardy's detached narrator describes "the atmosphere [as] being in such delicate equilibrium and so trans-missive that inanimate objects seemed endowed with two or three senses, if not five" (127), moving next to a description of the distasteful but not unlovely garden in which Tess moves:

> The outskirt of the garden . . . had been left uncultivated for some years, and was now damp and rank with juicy grass which sent up mists of pollen at a touch, and with tall blooming weeds emitting offensive smells—weeds whose red and yellow and purple hues formed a polychrome as dazzling as that of cultivated flowers. She went stealthily as a cat through this profusion of growth, gathering cuckoo-spittle on her skirts, cracking snails that were underfoot, staining her hands with thistle-milk and slug-slime, and rubbing off upon her naked arms sticky blights which, though snow-white on the appletree-trunks, made madder stains on her skin; thus she drew quite near to Clare, still unobserved of him. (127)

Hardy here repeats, and complicates, elements of two of the earlier episodes we have examined. The red, yellow, and purple weeds—so brilliant as to make them seem flowers—recall "the iridescence of coagulation" and "hundred prismatic hues" the morning sun produces in the blood of the dead horse Prince (37). Similarly, the "madder," that is, scarlet, stains on Tess's naked arms recall the crimson drops of blood that splash Tess from skirt to face when she attempts to stem the flow of blood from the dying Prince. Also Alec's deflowering of Tess—at once producing life and destroying it—that Hardy had imaged as the tracing of "a coarse pattern" upon "beautiful feminine tissue" he here reconfigures in the "staining" of Tess's flesh as she draws close to Angel, entranced by the sound of his music and his physical presence.

For Tess is passionately stirred by Angel, and thus she moves "stealthily as a cat" toward him:

> Tess was conscious of neither time nor space.... Exaltation ... came now without any determination of hers; she undulated upon the thin notes of the second-hand harp, and their harmonies passed like breezes through her, bringing tears into her eyes. The floating pollen seemed to be his notes made visible, and the dampness of the garden the weeping of the garden's sensibility. Though near nightfall, the rank-smelling weed-flowers glowed as if they would not close, for intentness, and the waves of colour mixed with the waves of sound. (127–28)

Attractive as he makes this beaugly scene in the garden at Talbothays—and critics continue to celebrate it as one of the great scenes in Hardy's fiction—it is difficult to ignore some rhetorical straining in his effort here to simulate beauty in ugliness. Hardy writes of inanimate objects endowed with senses; of abolition of near from far; of sound in soundlessness; of notes that move on the air as if they were unclothed; of grass that emits pollen-mists; of stinking weeds whose colors suggest (sweet-smelling) flowers; of sticky substances that produce whiteness on wood but scarlet stains on human flesh. Hardy's groping is the result in part of his use of inversion to exhibit and at the same time defer explaining the beaugly. Whereas in the death of Prince and the rape of Tess Hardy exhibited, respectively, beauty in the ugliness of violent death and sexual violation, here, at a moment of great happiness for Tess, he "inverts" his effort in order to uncover an ugliness in beauty.

Hardy repeats, and at the same time diverges from, the goring of

Rally as Defeat

Prince and the violation of Tess, by reconfiguring the critical image of trespass: the notes of Angel's music move "through her," and Hardy has her respond, as on the road to Casterbridge and in The Chase, with a flow of tears. Hardy diverges from the two previous episodes by depicting Tess for the first time as being capable of directing passion rather than simply responding to it.

Having discovered and directed anger at Alec and the two obtuse religionists, Tess has wakened through the beauty of the violence of anger to a way to approach this man who attracts her so strongly. How this occurs is revealed just a few pages later, when Angel courts Tess and assigns her the fanciful names Artemis and Demeter. Tess displays two of anger's fruits: resistance and self-assertion: "'Call me Tess,' she would say askance; and he did'" (135). Then, with the advancing light, Hardy quickly adds, "her [beautiful] features would become simply feminine; they had changed from those of a divinity who could confer bliss to those of a being who craved it" (135).

Tess's resistance to Angel's attempt, however fanciful, to give her the names of pagan goddesses, her gentle but firm determination to be known and loved by her given name, is another sign of her newfound power to resist, to assert, to have her way, so to speak, with this man she loves. This self-assertion is one path to recuperation, one way in which to rally from defeat. And in human terms, Tess is never so appealing as when she commands that the man whom she desperately loves call her by her given name. Her command has two sources: she craves a bliss she believes Angel can provide and she feels guilt about her past. She wants truth even more than she wants happiness. For Angel to call her Demeter (goddess of marriage and human fertility) or Artemis (goddess of the moon and the chase) rather than simply "Tess" (goddess of nothing whatsoever) is to blur reality, to destroy concrete identity by idealizing it.

This division in Tess is specially poignant because, as by now is clear, any appeal Hardy would ascribe to Tess exists as part of a terrible beauty with which he is informing her rapidly developing consciousness.

The aura surrounding romantic love has roots in the physical body as well as in images of serenity and beauty, but in evoking the beaugly in Tess's happiness in love, Hardy inverts conventional imagery to suggest that nature is monotonous and predictable, that evil lurks beneath pastoral beauty, that human beauty is transient and imperfect, and that what usually masquerades as idealized love can be reduced to irrepressible passion.

In a passage following Tess's assertion that Angel call her by her given name, Hardy continues to evoke ugliness in the apparently beautiful, describing the waterfowl that Tess and Angel observe: "At these non-human hours [Tess and Angel] could get quite close to the waterfowl. Herons came, with a great bold noise as of opening doors and shutters, out of the boughs of a plantation which they frequented at the side of the mead; or, if already on the spot, hardily maintained their standing in the water as the pair walked by, watching them by moving their heads in a slow, horizontal, passionless wheel, like the turn of puppets by clockwork" (135).

Hardy here uses a bird, a familiar poetic symbol for motion, freedom, and transcendence, to exact a sense of mechanism, monotony, even lifelessness. He imposes a similarly perverse image on the grazing cattle, a conventional symbol for pastoral tranquility: "On the grey moisture of the grass were marks where the cows had lain through the night—dark-green islands of dry herbage the size of their carcases in the general sea of dew. From each island proceeded a serpentine trail, by which the cow had rambled away to feed after getting up" (135). Hardy in-animates each cow by making it islandlike, then reanimates it, at the same time transmogrifying it from mammal to serpent. He re-creates even the trees, and Tess with them: "[T]he meadows lay like a white sea, out of which the scattered trees rose like dangerous rocks. . . . Minute diamonds of moisture from the mist hung, too, upon Tess's eye-lashes, and drops upon her hair, like seed pearls. When the day grew quite strong and commonplace these dried off her; moreover, Tess then lost her strange and ethereal beauty; her teeth, lips, and eyes scintillated in the sunbeams, and she was again the dazzlingly fair dairymaid only, who had to hold her own against the other women of the world" (135). Hardy punctuates this deflation of the divinely beautiful in Tess with a harsh-sounding human voice: Dairy-man Crick scolding the late-arriving milkers and rebuking one of them for not washing her hands: "For Heaven's sake, pop thy hands under the pump, Deb! Upon my soul, if the London folk only knowed of thee and thy slovenly ways, they'd swaller their milk and butter more mincing than they do a'ready" (135).

Even to the routine of meal making—evidence of a reassuring orderliness in this rural Eden—Hardy lends a dark hue. The sound of the heavy breakfast table being dragged from the wall in the kitchen is a "horrible scrape," another hint that the scenic beauties of Talbothays garb bleaker, more sombre beauties. Hardy even produces a burlesque, that is, a comically grotesque imitation of the beaugly when Angel, physically aroused by Tess's beauty, responds with a sneeze, a sneeze critics who take delight in the heightened language of this passage too often ignore.

> How very lovable her face was to him. Yet there was nothing ethereal about it: all was real vitality, real warmth, real incarnation. And it was in her mouth that this culminated. . . . To a young man with the least fire in him that little upward lift in the middle of her red top lip was distracting, infatuating, maddening. He had never before seen a woman's lips and teeth which forced upon his mind, with such persistent iteration, the old Elizabethan simile of roses filled with snow. Perfect, he, as a lover, might have called them off-hand. But no: they were not perfect. And it was the touch of the imperfect upon the would-be perfect that gave the sweetness, because it was that which gave the humanity.
>
> Clare had studied the curves of those lips so many times that he could reproduce them mentally with ease; and now, as they again confronted him, clothed with colour and life, they sent an *aura* over his flesh, a breeze through his nerves, which well-nigh produced a qualm; and actually produced by some mysterious physiological process, a prosaic sneeze. (152–53)

The sweetness of the defect in would-be perfection is precisely the beauty in ugliness Hardy seeks to convey, but here he makes it redolent not of a faintness produced by sexual arousal, but of a sneeze, an

"Achoo" of "mysterious physiological" origin, a mischievous reductive echo of Angel's idealizing love. As this should suggest, and as remarked earlier, it is a mistake to expect Hardy to provide final clarification of his play upon the beauty in the ugly and the ugly in the beautiful.

What is most striking about Hardy's rendering of Tess emerges when Angel Clare rejects Tess on the night of their wedding. At this critical point in the writing of his narrative, the point at which he turns the careers of both Tess and Angel in radically different directions, Hardy finds a way to place in their psyches different senses of the beaugly that he then uses to delineate the racking estrangement-in-marriage they know after Angel returns to Tess. What to this point in his narrative Hardy had used mainly as an atmospheric effect, he now is able to employ as a psychic one. He does this by locating beauty in that ugliest of human passions—hatred—and building there yet another home for the beaugly.

11

Hatred's Beauties

Hardy reverses the courses of the lives of Tess and Angel in a devastatingly simple way. Angel believes his new wife is a virgin and then discovers in self-righteous horror that she has borne a child out of wedlock: "My position is this. . . . I thought—any man would have thought—that by giving up all ambition to win a wife with social standing, with fortune, with knowledge of the world, I should secure rustic innocence, as surely as I should secure pink cheeks; but . . ." (234). Tess believes her new husband is forgiving (especially after he confesses to her a lapse equivalent to her own), but then she discovers, with equal horror, that he is unforgiving to an extreme:

> [Tess:] In the name of our love, forgive me. . . . I have forgiven you for the same. . . . Forgive me, as you are forgiven. *I* forgive *you*, Angel (226). . . .
> [Angel:] I do forgive you. But forgiveness is not all.
> [Tess:] And love me?
> To this question he did not answer. (229)

Angel's love for Tess, Tess's love for Angel, both thwarted, curdle into aversion; that aversion turns to hatred; the hatred turns back into love, but that love is chastened, made beaugliful by mutual hatred. The love for one another Angel and Tess know between the day she murders Alec and the day of her execution for that crime is love born of their having set aside the hatred caused by mutual betrayal. Love becoming hatred, hatred peering through love—this is the emotional origin of the severe beauty Hardy pursues in the second half of *Tess*.

Throughout, as my choice of the word "curdle" suggests, the interchange between love and hate is almost chemical, like the organic change in Prince's spilt blood that produces an instant of strange beauty on the road to Casterbridge. This beauty in reality-soured love (love soured by the revelation of unflattering realities) is the beaugliness Hardy depicts here. The souring of Tess and Angel's love reminds one of the way a trace of garlic in a pasture at Talbothays "turns," that is, chemically alters, the milk—rendering it unpalatable (142–43). But whereas the pungent garlic can be uprooted and the flavor of fresh milk restored, the roots of hatred are not so easily detected, and, when detected, not so easily pulled up; and so the recovery of freshness, of the uncritical loving Angel and Tess shared at Talbothays, is as impossible, as futile, as an attempt to restore Tess's virginity. It is ever thus in Hardy: there is no undoing the done, and singing the sadness in that grim truth's beauty is the object of much of his writing.

When Angel and Tess first meet on the green at Marlott, and again when they meet at Talbothays, each registers an aversion to the other. In the episode at Marlott, Angel is one of "three young men of a superior class" (21), the brothers Clare, who are on a holiday walking tour. They come upon the women of rural Marlott dressed in white, waiting for the men of their village to finish work for the day so that the May Day dancing can begin. The encounter between classes and sexes (rural, working-class women, and educated middle-class men) is focal to the entire story. Felix and Cuthbert Clare, Angel's elder brothers and both clergymen-to-be, want nothing to do with "a troop of country hoydens," that is, a group of carefree peasant women, because they think associating with such women is beneath the dignity of their station.

Angel, however, is "amused" by this group of women dancing

without male partners, and he decides to provide male companionship. He approaches them "gallantly," that is, flirtatiously and patronizingly, and in the manner of an Alec d'Urberville he asks archly, "Where are your partners, my dears?" (22) (compare Alec's remark to Tess, "What—my beauty—You here so late?" at the dance at Chaseborough shortly before he rapes her. [66]). Angel then surveys the group of dancers dressed in white and chooses one, not Tess, to favor with his company. Tess is offended by his failure to select her and looks disappointed. Angel recognizes her dismay and regrets his failure to choose her (for "she . . . looked so soft in her thin white gown" [23]), and then he hurries on his way.

Angel's cool choice of one from among "the bevy," his not bothering to learn her name, his noting Tess's bodily contours beneath her semitransparent garment—these gestures are socially and sexually based. It is unlikely that he would have approached a group of women of his own or of a superior class in such a manner. Angel acts like a client at a brothel, choosing his partner, satisfying his need, regretting he had not enjoyed a different partner, then hurrying off.

Because he is the only Clare male not to attain a university degree, because he has chosen to descend the social scale by deciding to learn farming, Angel has declassed himself, made of himself a social anomaly. In defense of this, he evinces "considerable indifference to social forms and observances," and he comes to despise "material distinctions of rank and wealth" (121). Living at Talbothays has awakened him to the astonishing fact that there are worthy and interesting human beings in the rural working class: "Much to his surprise he took . . . a real delight in their companionship" (122). He begins to take his meals with them, downstairs in the general dining room, rather than upstairs in his private quarters; but when he dines with them downstairs, he sits at a separate table.

In short, Angel Clare is an adolescent snob, rebelling against authority by slumming, or "lame-ducking" as it is sometimes termed, by associating with people of a social class with whom he would not normally associate, people who are inferior to him in culture and in station, people of whom he knows his parents would disapprove.

One of my teachers, the woman with whom I first studied *Tess* some 30 years ago, may have had Angel's rebellion in mind when she described him as "the great Mule of English literature." The metaphor is apt because a mule is neither an ass nor a horse, is known for stubbornness, and usually is unable to reproduce its kind. (Alec, in fact, at one point refers to Angel as "that mule.") But my teacher no doubt also saw in Angel a person destructively out of touch with his feelings; and of course by declassing himself, Angel fundamentally alienates himself from his feelings; for people's personal and social feelings (particularly their sexual feelings) derive directly from their sense of social and family identity and the values involved therein. How we love is closely connected with who we are as social beings. Although Angel does his best to suppress his social and family identity, and therefore his way of loving, he is ultimately unable to suppress his upbringing. That failure contributes to the death of his love for Tess, and the death of Tess herself.

Angel's first response to Tess upon encountering her at Talbothays reeks of snobbery and self-alienation. He overhears her speaking at mealtime and says to himself, "What a fluty voice one of those milkmaids has. I suppose it is the new one" (124). He responds here not to Tess as a person but as one of a class of faceless people ("one of those milkmaids"). As he listens to her speak further, he turns to observe her and (still) sees not an individual but another abstraction: "'What a fresh and virginal daughter of Nature that milkmaid is' . . . And then he seemed to discern in her something that was familiar, something which carried him back into a joyous and unforseeing past, before the necessity of taking thought had made the Heavens grey" (124).

Angel sees and hears in Tess an opiate for the pain of thinking, for the boredom of his desultory, anomalous existence. She is a cure for, a distraction from his uncertainty about his identity, yet another means of thwarting his parents' expectations for him. She is for him a means to an end, not an end in herself, a representative of a group, not an individual. When he speaks with Tess in the garden, shortly after first hearing her voice, he is "surprised" (128) to find this "daughter of nature" capable of serious thought: able to express "in her own native phrases—assisted a little by her sixth-standard training—feelings which might almost have been called those of the age—the ache of modernism" (129). She attracts him not because of what she is, or even what she says, but because she approximates something other, something intellectually interesting to him. He does not know how to approach this "daughter of the soil" (131), whose physical charm has his blood at a near boil, except to ask her whether she might not wish to "take up [a] course of study—history for example" (130). Study, he instinctively believes, is one thing that will elevate her to his middle station, even though he ostensibly deplores that station, its expectations and presumptions.

Of course, Angel's avowed disdain for fine ladies is nonsense, as he reveals when he visits his family shortly before the wedding and asks his straitlaced mother and father "What kind of wife do you think would be best for me, as a thrifty hard-working farmer?" He gets an answer: "a pure and saintly woman" (165). When his mother asks if Angel's intended is "of a family such as you would care to marry into—a lady, in short," Angel replies that his chosen one, though a cottager's daughter, "*is* a lady, nevertheless—in feeling and nature" (166). Later, contradicting his avowed disdain for aristocratic families, he will defend his choice of Tess because she is of the aristocratic d'Urbervilles; but later still, he contradicts his contradiction and upbraids Tess by suggesting that her lapse with Alec is the result of her derivation from the d'Urbervilles.

Given her experience with Alec, that other male of superior station slumming about the countryside as a would-be farmer, Tess is more canny than Angel about the danger of "unequal attachments" (134) such as the one she senses developing between Angel and herself. On the other hand, she has heard from the dairyman's wife that Angel might prefer a "farm-woman" to a "fine lady" (141). She also understands, because, as Hardy puts it, she is "woman enough" to do so, that Angel has "the honour of all the dairymaids in his keeping" (144), and she believes Angel is an honorable man.

When Tess is hovering between self-contempt and the growing

self-esteem of being loved, Hardy places her within hearing of Dairyman Crick's story of Jack Dollop (who had seduced a young woman but was brought to heel by the young woman's mother with the help of a butter-churn [137–38]). This comic version of Tess's tragic story, this amusing version of her painful experience, induces in Tess a flash of the beaugly. Suddenly, as on the road from Trantridge to Marlott, she sees ordinary things utterly differently. Hardy uses his detached observer to invoke Tess's glimpse of beaugliness through metaphor: "The evening sun was now ugly to her, like a great inflamed wound in the sky. Only a solitary cracked-voiced reed-sparrow greeted her from the bushes by the river, in a sad, machine-like tone, resembling that of a past friend whose friendship she had outworn" (139).

Yet if Tess is more canny than Angel about the dangers of crossing class lines in love and marriage, she is also blinded to these very dangers by Angel's superior endowments. She has never before known a man of his qualities: "There was hardly a touch of earth in her love for Clare. To her sublime trustfulness he was all that goodness could be, knew all that a guide, philosopher, and friend should know. She thought every line in the contour of his person the perfection of masculine beauty; his soul the soul of a saint; his intellect that of a seer. The wisdom of her love for him, as love, sustained her dignity; she seemed to be wearing a crown. The compassion of his love for her, as she saw it, made her lift up her heart to him in devotion" (193).

Tess and Angel idealize one another because neither is able to see the other as an individual possessing both vices and virtues. This inability stems from unbridgeable differences of education, taste, and perception, that is, differences of class.

As they mount the stairs to their bedchamber on the wedding night, which by Angel's choice they are to spend in a house once occupied by a branch of the d'Urbervilles, Tess is moved less by the anticipation of the consummation of their love than by life-sized portraits of two "horrid women" embedded in panels in the masonry—d'Urberville women who had lived two centuries before: "The long pointed features, narrow eye, and smirk of the one, so suggestive of merciless treachery; the bill-hook nose, large teeth, and bold eye of the other, suggesting arrogance to the point of ferocity" (214). Especially unsettling for Angel is his sense that his bride's "fine features were unquestionably traceable in these exaggerated forms" (215). Angel trembles before a palimpsest, another instance of beaugliness: the lovely features of his beloved Tess overlay the horrid features of two of her female ancestors; her beauty masks their ugliness, and their ugliness peers through her beauty. Later, after Tess has told him of her past, he looks into the face of another of these Tess-like witches, this one in the masonry over the entrance of Tess's bedchamber. Then, his hatred for Tess fully awake, he sees "sinister design [and] . . . a concentrated purpose of revenge on the other sex" (231) in a portrait that, even more than before, resembles his bride.

Before Tess makes her confession to Angel, she dreams dreams of well-being, because she believes that Angel will forgive her lack of innocence. Hardy depicts her hope before confessing and her hopelessness afterward by describing the fire that burns in their bedchamber grate. In the fire that burns with Tess's hope there are warm embers: "A steady glare from the now flameless embers painted the sides and back of the fireplace with its colour, and the well-polished andirons, and the old brass tongs that would not meet. The underside of the mantel-shelf was flushed with the high-coloured light, and the legs of the table nearest the fire. Tess's face and neck reflected the same warmth, which each gem turned into an Aldebaran or Sirius—a constellation of white, red, and green flashes, that interchanged their hues with her every pulsation" (220).

It is as if the prospect of receiving absolution from the man-god she loves has transported Tess into the starry heavens, the mythic home of the gods, or better, as if the spiritual emblem of the heavenly has suffused Tess herself. As Hardy readies Tess to tell her story, however, he transforms this fire—the source of warm comfort—into an inferno:

> The ashes under the grate were lit by the fire vertically, like a torrid waste. Imagination might have beheld a Last-Day luridness in this red-coaled flow, which fell on his face and hand, and on hers, peer-

ing into the loose hair about her brow, and firing the delicate skin underneath. A large shadow of her shape rose upon the wall and ceiling. She bent forward, at which each diamond on her neck gave a sinister wink like a toad's; and pressing her forehead against his temple she entered on her story of her acquaintance with Alec d'Urberville and its results. (222)

Hardy's deftest stroke in writing this episode was not to relate Tess's telling the story of her ruin. This restraint—this not writing—is as effective here as is his not writing a blow-by-blow account of her violation or her execution. His detached narrator simply says that she "murmur[s] the words without flinching, and with her eyelids drooping down" (222). She speaks to Angel in even tones, without "exculpatory phrase" and without weeping. Her self-control here, her refusal to make a special plea, indicates her trust in Angel and in the success of her rally.

Hardy chose to require the reader to fill in Tess's account because, as always, he wants his reader to trace the interchange between beauty and the other than beautiful, in this case the interchange between the beauty of love and the ugliness of hate.

Hardy focuses his marvelously appropriate language on describing the change in Tess and Angel's situation, first by using conditionals: things "seemed to suffer transmutation," "the fire looked impish . . . as if it did not care"; then he shifts to declaratives: "light . . . was engaged," "objects announced," "nothing had changed," "the essence . . . had changed" (225). And this final declaration rings true: a change in the "essence" of things has, from the beginning of their relationship, been latent in Angel's and Tess's antipathy, as well as in their strongly idealized love for each other. They are poised to enact the strange beauties available to the haters in love.

No doubt seeing the life-sized depictions of Tess's mighty ancestors reminds Angel of Tess's family's diminished status, for Angel has a viciously class-conscious response to Tess's attempt to plead her case to him after her confession:

[Angel:] 'Don't, Tess; don't argue. Different societies different manners. You almost make me say you are an unapprehending

peasant woman, who have [sic] never been initiated into the proportions of social things. You don't know what you say.'

[Tess:] 'I am only a peasant by position, not by nature.' She spoke
with an impulse to anger, but it went as it came.

[Angel:] 'So much the worse for you. . . . I cannot help associating your decline as a family with this other fact—of your want of
firmness. Decrepit families imply decrepit wills, decrepit conduct.'
(229)

Tess's discovery of this beauty of hate breeds the lethal hate that
finally destroys her. Nearly a year after she parts with Angel, Tess is
on a road leading away from her native Marlott. By this time she is a
nearly penniless vagabond seeking employment, "a lonely woman with
a basket and a bundle, in her own porterage" (266). Upon meeting on a
lonely stretch of the road a man who recognizes her and reminds her of
her past, she flees to a nearby woodland. Hardy reenacts yet again certain
terms of the scene of her rape in another dark wood, but with a most
significant difference. Again Tess lies in darkness in a heap of leaves
beneath the trees, but this time she is in no danger of being violated by
a man; instead she is at the mercy of her own self-destructive thoughts.
Her rest is interrupted not by a human intruder but by the sounds of
birds mortally wounded by hunters and left to die: "Sometimes it was a
palpitation, sometimes a flutter; sometimes it was a sort of gasp or gur-
gle" (270), the detached narrator observes. The plight of these creatures
reminds Tess of her own, and therefore she feels she must end their
suffering. Weeping, she introduces the beauty of mercy into death
by killing the birds "tenderly" (271). At the same time, she despises
herself for, in the words of the moralizing narrator, "her gloom, . . .
based on nothing more tangible than a sense of condemnation under
an arbitrary law of society which had no foundation in Nature" (271).
This observation on Tess's condition is less compelling than his detached narrator's observation ("Several pheasants lay about, their rich
plumage dabbled with blood" [271]) because Tess's killing the birds is
not so tender an act as the moralizer would purport it to be. Her
breaking the birds' necks rather than attempting to nurse them recalls
her flirtation with suicide (by hanging) shortly after Angel has rejected
her. In her killing the wounded birds with her bare hands one after

another, in her feeling directly and repeatedly through her hands and wrists her power to crush their vertebrae and end their lives, especially since she identifies with the misery of the birds, she is transforming self-hatred into lethal hatred for others. When Tess victimizes the birds, however tenderly, she vengefully enacts her sense of her own victimization. The woman who baptized her dying child has become the woman who can kill with her bare hands. She is the same woman, one recalls, who had joined in the slaughter of animals in the course of the harvest. Hardy does not separate the woman of exquisite beauty of spirit and the woman who is an agent of death; nor does he suggest that the latter destroys the former.

Later, when Tess is performing the brutal labor required of her at Flintcomb-Ash farm, she feels "like a bird caught in a clap-net" (282). But harried as she is then by the men in her life—the absent Angel, the boorish Farmer Groby, and Alec, who now reappears—she is not passive or abject, certainly not the ruined woman of literary convention. When Alec throws over his newly found religious faith and offers to marry her, she staunchly refuses. And when he insults Angel ("that mule you call husband" [320]), Tess retaliates by smashing her heavy leather glove against his mouth and spilling *his* blood.

Tess also retaliates against Angel in two ways: she writes him two letters of rebuke, and she eventually rejoins Alec. Tess's letters to her faraway husband have not received the attention they deserve as instruments of anger and expressions of her unorthodox beauty; in terms of their emotional violence they are more than the equivalent of her blow to Alec's face. In the first letter to Angel, Tess in effect repeats the plea for forgiveness she had made on their wedding night, but now with new urgency, because she is "exposed to temptation" (325–26) by Alec's renewed attentions (see also page 358). She contradicts her earlier words to Angel by saying now that the punishment he has "measured out" is "deserved . . . well deserved" (325). She asks now not for justice but for kindness. She assures him that he need not fear "a word of sting or bitterness from her," sure evidence that she harbors precisely such words. She assures him as well that she is not the woman he thinks she is but rather the better woman she has become under his influence—"another woman, filled full of new life from you" (325). Then she writes an astonishing sentence, precisely the kind of sentence an overly indulgent mother might write to condone the worst behavior of, that is, to spoil, an intractable child: "Dear, if you would only be a little more conceited, and believe in yourself so far as to see that you were strong enough to work this change in me, you would perhaps be in a mind to come to me, your poor wife" (325). This backhanded compliment stems from desperation, and her desperation soon spills over into bitter resentment: "Ah, if I could only make your dear heart ache one little minute of each day as mine does every day and all day long, it might lead you to show pity to your poor lonely one" (325).

Just as, earlier, Tess deflected hatred for Angel and Alec onto the wounded birds by "tenderly" breaking their necks, she later deflects her wish to make Angel's heart ache by driving a knife into Alec's heart. For Alec is much on her mind in this letter, not just because, as she will later tell Angel, Alec has been as a husband to her, but also because Alec wants her to be his wife. Alec, we must remember, responded to her blow to his mouth, not with another blow, not even with furious words, but with this telling remark: "You most unjustly forget one thing, that I would have married you if you had not put it out of my power to do so. Did I not ask you flatly to be my wife—hey?—answer me." Tess acknowledges the truth of his remark: "You did" (321).

When Tess finally gives way to Alec's pleadings, she writes a second letter to Angel, as brief as the earlier was lengthy, and as bitterly angry as the earlier was conciliatory: "O why have you treated me so monstrously, Angel! I do not deserve it. I have thought it all over carefully, and I can never, never forgive you ! You know that I did not intend to wrong you—why have you so wronged me? You are cruel, cruel indeed! I will try to forget you. It is all injustice I have received at your hands" (343). There will be no more indulgence from Tess. The beauty in hatred, born of unmerited suffering, is evident in the force and clarity of Tess's seven terse sentences, particularly in her emphatic self-assertions and in her accusatory and remonstrative statements.

The beauty in ugliness in Tess's angry letters to Angel is more apparent because her writing deepens the reality of her hatred in love for Angel. In writing she addresses Angel in terms that are more fundamental and less evanescent than the terms of her speech on the wedding night. Her second, angry letter to Angel echoes, and reverses, her begging forgiveness on the wedding night. Whereas she had earlier begged forgiveness of him in person, she now writes him that she refuses to forgive him. In the earlier letter she had placed beneath Angel's door (and accidentally under a carpet) at Talbothays, she had offered explanation, but she now implicitly demands explanation.

In writing, Tess inscribes her hatred into the records of humankind. She leaves personal evidence of her connection with and claim on Angel, a connection and claim confirmed by the marriage license, the official document so easily set aside by Angel on behalf of his wounded idealism. The two letters are more lasting, more punitive, records of her struggle than any of her spoken words or acts because they can be read over and over, they can be read by others, used by others to hold Angel accountable, used by Angel (as they are) to hold himself accountable. By writing out her anger and sense of injustice, Tess departs from the merely personal realm of speech and enters the collective, and therefore preexisting, realm of written language. Inscribed upon by Alec because she was passive and unresisting, inscribed upon by Angel because she was worshipful of his attainments, Tess has reached the point where she can inscribe on Angel emotional recrimination, as she will later direct violence at Alec, though with a knife rather than a pen. As Alec wounded her, so she will wound him; as Angel instructed her, so she here indicts him.

Actually, her angry missive to Angel might well have been directed at Alec, for its language as easily describes his physical assault on her as it does Angel's ideological assault on her. Tess's angry letter, written hard on the heels of Alec's renewed plea that she allow him to support her and her family—a plea to which she responds by crunching his arm between the casement and the stone mullion of a window—is her covert announcement to Angel that she must, out of material and emotional necessity, turn to Alec.

Hatred's Beauties

The terms of Tess's emotional need are complex, as Hardy suggests in the strikingly beaugliful garden in chapter 50. Having returned to nurse her ailing mother, Tess finds she must also cultivate the family garden, lest the family be wholly without provisions. As she along with other work people burns dead weeds, Alec, in the guise of Satan, rises up before her and tempts her in the garden plot. As in earlier episodes of beaugliness, it is twilight, a twilight thickened here not by a fog or a mist but by the pungent smoke of burning couch grass and cabbage stalks.

Characteristically, Hardy attempts to unveil the negative beauty in this moment of transmission. The sounds, sights, smells of the garden—all eerily pleasing—are his primary concern, so his vantage point is that of his observing narrator:

> [O]n one of the couch-burning plots . . . [Tess] laboured with her fork, its four shining prongs resounding against the stones and dry clods in little clicks. Sometimes she was completely involved in the smoke of her fire; then it would leave her figure free, irradiated by the brassy glare from the heap. She was oddly dressed to-night, and presented a somewhat staring aspect, her attire being a gown bleached by many washings, with a short black jacket over it, the effect of the whole being that of a wedding and funeral guest in one". (335)

Hardy prevents our seeing Tess's misery—as she works she thinks either of her distant husband or her ailing family—apart from the dark beauties of the scene; nor does he write beauty into this scene in order to mock Tess's misery. The dark attractions of the viscous village night, "the fantastic mysteries of light and shade" (336), are an integral part of Tess's complicated (both "wedding" and "funeral") state of mind. And so, a "pale opalescence" from the sky, another echo of "that iridescence of coagulation" in the blood on the road to Casterbridge, reveals a subdued, severe beauty.

Out of this mixture of darkness and light Alec rises, wearing the clothing of a laborer but quoting Milton like a theology student: "A jester might say this is just like Paradise. You are Eve, and I am the old other one, come to tempt you in the guise of an inferior animal" (336). Hardy shapes this scene, whose "grotesqueness" he remarks upon, with explicit literary reference (to John Milton's *Paradise Lost*), thereby echoing the encounter between Angel and Tess at Talbothays, where he had called attention to their Eden-like situation (134). If readers did not know otherwise, they might think that the garden at Talbothays was Tess's paradise and the garden at Marlott Tess's inferno. But the tangle of Tess's feelings at this point suggests otherwise. If Tess now hates the Angel she learned to love at Talbothays, she is also moving toward the devil she learned to hate in the Chase, the devil whose arm she bruises in a window casement, the devil whose mistress she will soon become, the devil whom she will stab to death.

Alec wins Tess back because he expresses concern for the well-being of her family, also because she is desperately lonely, in terminal need of sexual companionship. "I have no husband," she tells him with bitter humiliation (337). Just as Hardy elided the details of the encounter in the Chase, he omits here the details of Tess's decision to return to Alec, her moment of concession, the words they must have spoken, the precise nature of their renewed relationship.

Hardy termed "Fulfilment" the last phase of Tess's career, but in the ordinary sense of the word, Tess's last days are no more truly fulfilling than her days at Talbothays were a true rallying. Tess's fulfilment is really an emptying out, an utter depletion of her spirit, the end of the process that began when Angel rejected her. Tess's depletion is signalled by Hardy's abandonment of the moral and detached narrators who have been instrumental in evoking the beaugly in favor of Angel Clare's consciousness. Therefore, neither Tess's reunion with Angel nor the scene at Stonehenge contain the strange beauty that had suffused the fateful episodes that have led up to the final phase of the novel.

Driven by the rebuke of him in Tess's impassioned letter Angel tracks her to The Herons, a stylish hotel at a fashionable watering place, where Tess lives in luxury as Alec's mistress. From the moment of their meeting here to the moment of her arrest by the police at

Stonehenge (381–82), Tess is a shadow of her former self, a vacancy: without anger, without hatred, bent with near madness. Her actions lack the strange beauty that had accompanied her actions since the collision on the road to Casterbridge.

When Angel and Tess meet again, Hardy endows Tess with mere beauty of fashionable dress, beauty that, like the conventional beauty of scenery, he rejects as false because it is founded on a false notion of the actual condition of men and women. In other episodes he displaces Tess's natural beauty with a negative beauty, a beauty more in keeping with the tragic sombreness and obscurity of her condition, but he does not do so here. Similarly, Hardy cannot delineate an unorthodox beauty in the famous Stonehenge scene (379 ff), in which he returns Tess to the locale of her maternal ancestors to die as if she were a sacrificial victim. In the Stonehenge scene, impressive set piece that it is, Hardy merely juxtaposes, does not fuse, unlikes. Here the "fantastic mysteries of light and shade" (336) that are so important in the evocation of the beaugly, are not transmissive, and therefore they are neither fantastic nor mysterious. Tess's bequeathing Liza-Lu to Angel, Angel's refusal to indulge Tess's pathetic belief that they will reunite in spirit after their deaths, even her staunch "I am ready" to the police who appear out of nowhere—none of these actions so much as intimates the severe beauty Hardy has led us to expect at such moments of heightened emotion throughout his novel. He is reaching, unsuccessfully, for such a beauty in a passage such as the following:

> The band of silver paleness along the east horizon made even the distant parts of the Great Plain appear dark and near; and the whole enormous landscape bore that impress of reserve, taciturnity, and hesitation which is usual just before day. The eastward pillars and their architraves stood up blackly against the light, and the great flame-shaped Sun-stone beyond them, and the stone of sacrifice midway. Presently the night wind died out, and the quivering little pools in the cup-like hollows of the stones lay still. (381)

What is absent here is the use of the language of paradox and metaphor (the usages of his detached narrator at his best) to suggest those transmissive movements in which unlikes commingle to signal the new beauty: for example, the bloodied paleness of Tess's face mirroring the whiteness of the blood-spattered road; the serpentine movement of cattle across a dewy meadow; a sexual assault as an inscribing of a blank page; the superimposition of contrasting architectural design upon human form; a peasant woman in the role of a priest. There is no beaugliness in this episode because Hardy allows Angel Clare's consciousness to dominate. And that consciousness, because it resists mystery, banishes transmutative thought, forbids trespass, and therefore denies the possibility that beauty might dwell anywhere in the neighborhood of ugliness or imperfection.

12

Angel Clare:
Beauty Dwells Where Perfection Lives

Hardy's wish to reveal beauty in ugliness in *Tess* is a major effort in characterization, especially in respect to his depiction of Angel Clare, a character much neglected, or, when not neglected, much maligned, by readers of the novel. Angel is often dismissed as incompletely realized, or as unattractive—to his author as well as to the reader. Some readers may feel that Hardy does not satisfactorily account for Angel's tendency to live by stern moral scruples when sympathy would be the more merciful response to human suffering. Hardy's supposed difficulty in bringing Angel to life is sometimes attributed to Angel being a partial self-portrait, a figure on whom Hardy could not gain sufficient distance to portray convincingly.

On the other hand, when one considers Angel in the context of Hardy's effort to display the working of the beaugly, it is clear that Hardy sets up Angel to see in Tess, for the most compellingly intimate reasons, the beauty of defect, but then, finally, only ugliness, deficiency, and failure. That is, Angel is a study in thwarted sympathy, a study in hobbled imagination. He is interesting because he is haunted by some of the same questions we have been asking throughout this book: How can there be beauty in ugliness? Of what practical value is it to set aside moral judgment in the interest of beauty when faced with violence, death, cruelty, hatred, or other extreme circumstances? Is it not inhumane to even look for beauty in such events?

Hardy moves Angel through his inner debate first by portraying his abandonment of Tess after he discovers (on his wedding night) that Tess is not pure, then, second, by having Angel reason his way toward loving acceptance of Tess after long absence from her, and finally, by having him retract this acceptance upon discovering that Tess has renewed her relationship with Alec.

Perhaps the most revealing episode of Angel's overly thoughtful life occurs shortly after he has decided to abandon Tess, when, on his way to he knows not where, he unexpectedly meets Izz Huett, one of Tess's companions from Talbothays. Izz has long loved Angel, and Angel has been aware of her interest in him. For a moment, Angel flirts with the notion of taking up with Izz, of inviting her to accompany him on his travels: "[Clare] was incensed against his fate, bitterly disposed towards social ordinances; for they had cooped him up in a corner out of which there was no legitimate pathway. Why not be revenged on society by shaping his future domesticities loosely, instead of kissing the pedagogic rod of convention in this ensnaring manner?" (263). Angel goes so far as to ask Izz to join him in his cart, and they drive together for two miles. Angel asks Izz if she loves him more than Tess does, to which Izz replies, "No, . . . not more than she. . . . Because nobody could love 'ee more than Tess did! . . . She would have laid down her life for 'ee. I could do no more!" (263).

Izz's honesty about Tess's love causes Angel to turn back on his decision to make Izz his companion, and he does this at great pain to himself and even greater pain to poor Izz. But though renewed knowledge of Tess's extraordinary love for him prevents his "impulse toward folly and treachery" (264), it does not turn him back to Tess, though he was "within a feather-weight's turn" (265) of doing so. He has no "contempt for her nature, nor the probable state of her heart" (265); rather, it is his sense that "despite her love as corroborated by Izz's admission, the facts had not changed. If he was right at first, he was right now" (265). His love for Tess, unlike Tess's love for him, is not strong enough to transform the ugly fact of her prior sexual experience. He cannot think of who Tess is because he cannot set aside what she has done.

At the root of this stubbornness is Angel's need to cling emotionally and socially to values and practices that he finds intellectually inadequate. He has set aside the supernatural aspects of Christian theology but, without being fully aware of it, he clings to some of the more mystical aspects of Christian morality, particularly the notion that sexual purity is an apex of virtue, especially female virtue: "With all his attempted independence of judgment this advanced and well-meaning young man, a sample product of the last five-and -twenty years, was yet the slave to custom and conventionality when surprised back to her early teachings" (258). Once Angel has seen the stupidity in deserting Tess because she had borne a child out of wedlock, it should be simple for him to reunite with her, no matter what her circumstances. But he finds it impossible because his traditional feelings and tastes are stronger than his liberated ideas. He cannot find satisfaction in a woman whose condition he knows his family, with their stern sense of respectability, would deplore. Like them, "in considering what Tess was not he overlooked what she was, and forgot that the defective can be more than the entire" (259).

So Hardy cannot plausibly portray Angel as capable of changing his mind about the possibility that beauty dwells where ugliness of moral defect lives, because then Angel would have to forget entirely his puritanical reason for rejecting Tess. For an idealist like Angel, forgiving is a humane ideal in its own right; forgetting, however, is something entirely different. He cannot forget Tess's past, cannot shake free of his obsession with "freshness" because, as Tess shrewdly tells him, "It is in your own mind, what you are angry at, Angel; it is not in me" (229). Tess is only half right, for Angel is actually both angry about what Tess has done and victimized by the way he thinks.

Angel later thinks himself into forgiveness of Tess's impurity: "[Angel's] . . . parochialism made him ashamed. . . . His inconsistencies rushed upon him like a flood. He had persistently elevated Hellenic Paganism at the expense of Christianity; yet in that civilization an illegal [sexual] surrender was not certain disesteem. Surely then he might have regarded that abhorrence of the un-intact state, which he had inherited with the creed of mysticism, as at least open to correction when the result was due to treachery" (329–30).

Angel is allowing that Tess's loss of virginity is forgivable because it was a result of Alec's deceit, particularly because among the pagan Greeks illicit sexuality was allowable in certain circumstances. Angel has a habit, as we will note below, of testing his personal views against the historical record, as *he* knows and understands it. In spite of his apparent change of mind, however, Angel will fail Tess again, and he fails her because he continues to idealize her, cannot help judging her ruthlessly in terms of a system of values according to which imperfection is a vice; and vice is certainly not beautiful, nor is it the source of or occasion for beauty. Because Angel needs to love Tess as an epitomy of innocence and purity he can never completely bring himself to forgive and thereby to admit to her human imperfections. So Angel thinks, but only thinks, he can see in Tess a beauty (of loving loyalty) where formerly he had seen only the ugliness of impurity.

In Angel's apparent change toward Tess, Hardy suggests that Angel is trying to embrace the contradictions inherent in the beaugly, the beauty in ugliness, much as Hardy does with the technique of split narration—the virtual dialogue he effects between a moral and a detached, aesthetic view of Tess. Hardy exposes this struggle when Angel rethinks the morality of "the old systems of mysticism":

> He thought they wanted readjusting. Who was the moral man? Still more pertinently, who was the moral woman? The beauty or ugliness of a character lay not only in its achievements, but in its aims and impulses; its true history lay, not among things done, but among things willed.
>
> How, then, about Tess?
>
> Viewing [Tess] in these lights, a regret for his hasty judgment began to oppress him. Did he reject her eternally, or did he not? He could no longer say that he would always reject her, and not to say that was in spirit to accept her now (328–29).

Angel thinks he has changed his mind because he thinks he can learn to value what Tess can become, her possibilities, rather than what she has been, her past. Her error is not permanent, he believes, not fixed once and for all by unchangeable events; the beauty or ugliness of her life is relative to her changing desire, he thinks, relative to her ability to impose her will on circumstances. Of course, this is nonsense. Angel, a puritan by nurture and perhaps by nature, driven by remorse and moral cowardice, has simply swung round temporarily to a mild form of moral liberalism, "mild as milk," as one of Hardy's rustics might say. He is pretending that Tess can live her life wholly uninfluenced by past experiences that are still very much alive in her memory and, equally important, in the memories of others.

After all, the "innocent" Tess whom Angel had learned to love at Talbothays would not have been that particular Tess had she not encountered Alec d'Urberville, had she not borne, baptized, and buried a bastard son and then set out to make a new life for herself. The quality of her love for Angel is colored deeply by those events and the pain surrounding them. When Tess attempts to create a new life for herself, she must unavoidably take paths to some degree determined by her troubled past. For the new, whether in life or in art, is never totally original; it is always to a large degree divergent from things that already exist, and therefore the new is always significantly shaped, colored, even named by what already exists. This is the point, in part, of Hardy's use of the celebrated phrase "a pure woman" as subtitle for his novel. As a woman Tess can be pure only in terms of her particular experiences; that is, she can be chaste but not virginal. Hers then is not the purity of a beautiful innocence, but the purity of ugly experiences, something one perhaps might wish to term a higher innocence, because an innocence she has sought and forged rather than inherited. Therefore, her beauty is one that can please, and please profoundly, but never in conventional terms. The phrase "pure woman," meaning "woman pure with unavoidable impurity," is but another of Hardy's metaphors for the beaugly.

For the same reason that Tess is fenced in by her past, Angel is bound by his. He tries to counter his inbred ideas of morality by becoming loving and forgiving, but they are not so easy to change. So long as he is under the influence of remorse (spurred by the language of Tess's letters) and feels a somewhat smug self-satisfaction in having thought his way into an enlightened view of Tess, Angel seems prepared to judge Tess "constructively rather than biographically, by the will rather than by the deed" (357), as is illustrated in the following extraordinarily allusive passage: "He had undergone some strange experiences in his absence [from England]; he had seen the virtual Faustina in the literal Cornelia, a spiritual Lucretia in a corporeal Phryne; he had thought of the woman taken and set in the midst as one deserving to be stoned, and of the wife of Uriah being made a queen" (357). For Angel to see "the virtual Faustina" in "the literal Cornelia" he would need to see an unfaithful wife (Faustina was the notoriously unfaithful wife of a Roman emperor) in a truly faithful one (Cornelia, the wife of another prominent Roman, refused to marry after her husband's death); that is, he would have to see the ugliness of marital infidelity in the beauty of marital loyalty. Seeing "a spiritual Lucretia" in "a corporeal Phryne" would mean seeing the spirit of a legendarily devoted wife (Lucretia committed suicide after being raped) in the body of a Greek courtesan (Phryne was the lover of Praxiteles); that is, seeing fanatical wifely devotion in harlotry. For him to think of the woman taken to be stoned for adultery in John 8:3–7, he would have to remember Jesus' statement on that occasion to the scribes and Pharisees, those stern, hypocritical enforcers of the Jewish law: "He that is without sin among you, let him first cast a stone at her." Finally, in considering the enthronement of the wife of Uriah, Angel is recalling King David's adultery with Bathsheba and the cruel King's arranging to have Uriah killed in order to free Bathsheba to be his queen (2 Sam. 11).

In this passage Hardy reveals Angel's attempts to discover beaugliness in Tess. In thinking of Faustina/Cornelia and Lucretia/Phyrne, Angel is thinking, historically, of the way moral beauty and moral ugliness have cohabited, the way in which apparent beauty has been actual ugliness, and virtual ugliness actual beauty. In thinking of Jesus' rebuke to the enforcers of strict moral law, Angel is perhaps thinking self-critically, placing himself among those violent hypocrites, those stern enforcers of law who are unprepared to see potential beauty in any divergence from the law.

In thinking of David and Bathsheba, however, Angel is not being wholly self-critical. In equating himself with a king who makes an adulteress his queen after having her husband killed, and equating Tess with an adulteress (Bathsheba) elevated by the love of a king, Angel flirts with a view of himself as a law unto himself, and with a view of Tess as a mere instrument of his will. In casting about in these sentences for precedents in history and legend for the change he might depict in Angel, Hardy shows Angel undermining his wish to find beauty in the ugliness of Tess's moral failure. In the very allusions Angel selects to document the possibility of such a change, he exposes his inability to make such a change.

Angel's counterparts in each historical instance—the husbands of Faustina and Cornelia, and of Lucretia and Phryne, the men who would stone the woman taken in adultery, the regal lover of Bathsheba—are all men who either judge, that is, decide the fates of the women involved, or who enforce the standard by which their women are judged. The women in these historical instances are all the possessions of, at best the inferiors of the men. These women are judged by their relationships to men: Faustina and Phryne are legendary for their infidelity, Cornelia and Lucretia for their fidelity—to men; the adulterous woman who is about to be stoned has violated her duty to her husband, and Bathsheba, enthroned and possessed by a king, has been unfaithful to her husband.

Angel's mental world is emphatically a male world, so because Tess is willing to oppose, even attack, men and to assume male roles, her behavior exceeds the categories of Angel's well-stocked masculine mind, which seems to contain no celebrated historical instances of a man's loyalty to a woman, and certainly none of a man's disloyalty to a woman. At the same time that Hardy depicts Angel's growing enlightenment, then, Hardy depicts Angel's cultural understanding betraying him. Angel's understanding is faithful to the silences of history, legend, and sacred scripture regarding the experience of women. For history, legend, and scripture—like the fate of Tess—are the inscriptions of male consciousness. So when Tess "writes back," she does so in the language of men; and when she actively fights back, as when she derides the painter of biblical texts, as when she shouts at the village clergyman, as when she baptizes her child, and as when she bloodies Alec's face, and later drives a knife into Alec's heart, she does so in the manner of men. Yet Angel can see her actions only as crazed.

It is worth recalling here that the tragic story of Tess is a story of male predation and stupidity: the stupidity of her father and the clergyman who sets her father to dreaming of past family glories; the unwholesome schemes of the designing Alec; the warped messages of the ardently evangelical painter of signs; the small-mindedness of the pastor of Marlott who consigns her child to burial with the damned; the brutality of farmer Groby at Flintcomb; the unquestioning swift punishment of the authorities who apprehend, try, and execute her; the injustice of the (male) gods, Christian and Pagan, who sport with her fate. Even Dairyman Crick, otherwise so kindly toward Tess, when telling the story of Jack Dollop, despoiler of a maiden brought to justice by an angry mother, belongs to this group of stupid, domineering, or predatory males. How, then, can we expect Angel Clare to deviate from the norm, no matter how much Hardy tries to portray Angel as a different breed of man?

Angel is different—at least until he sees Tess on the stairs of a fashionable hotel at Sandbourne, in a cashmere dressing gown and slippers, her hands "once rosy, . . . now white and more delicate." Upon catching sight of this Tess and hearing her anguished "[Alec] has won me back—to him," Angel "flag[s] like one plague-stricken" (366). His first impulse is to assume responsibility ("Ah—it is my fault!" [366]) and thereby perhaps he tries to muster the courage to see a Cornelia in this Faustina, a Lucretia in this Phryne, perhaps to think of what Tess can become rather than what Tess has been. Here Angel has an opportunity to act on his insight into the sources of the beaugly, to see and celebrate the beaugly and not become like one of the crowd that stones the adulteress. Unfortunately, Angel is incapable of grasping the beauty in the ugliness of Tess's changed situation, perhaps because there is no beaugliness there, perhaps because he could not acknowledge it if it were there. He simply cannot practice what he has so very recently preached to himself. He has travelled from Brazil to England, then travelled about England, filled with the conviction that he can forgive, but when offered the opportunity, he cannot forgive.

Angel Clare: Beauty Dwells Where Perfection Lives

Although Angel does not run off again to Brazil, or Texas, he does something more vicious: he decides that Tess is mad. He is convinced, and it is in his deepest interest to be so convinced, "that his original Tess had spiritually ceased to recognize the body before him as hers—allowing it to drift, like a corpse upon the current, in a direction dissociated from its living will" (366). He cannot believe Tess deliberately and rationally chose to become Alec's mistress, even though he has Tess's letters as evidence. He believes she must be mad to have done such a thing. The superior Angel, the petitioning Tess—their situation is what it has ever been, in spite of his declaration of renewed, enlightened love. Tess, blind (or discerning?) with love, is too mad, presumably, to see ugliness in his "worn and unhandsome" face; instead she sees beauty in his ugliness on the day that she kills Alec: "Worn and unhandsome as he had become it was plain that she did not discern the least fault in his appearance. To her he was, as of old, all that was perfection, personally and mentally. He was still her Antinous, her Apollo even; his sickly face was beautiful as the morning to her affectionate regard on this day no less than when she first beheld him; for was it not the face of the one man on earth who had loved her purely, and who had believed in her as pure?" (373). On the other hand, Angel sees Tess as mad, unbalanced, an aberrant d'Urberville; he is capable of being her protector and no more. Her violent impulse is to him "very terrible, if true: if a temporary hallucination, sad" (373). He is too sane, presumably, to see beauty in her "mad grief."

Angel, to be sure, becomes Tess's companion after she has murdered Alec, and presumably her loving husband, for the brief remainder of her life. They flee Sandbourne together and enjoy a few tranquil days of intimacy at Bramshurst Court together. He even declares his love for her, though in the same breath he qualifies his tenderness: "I do love you Tess—O I do—it is all come back! . . . But how do you mean—you have killed him?" (372). "I love you, but . . ."—such is the rhetoric of one for whom beauty dwells only where perfection lives.

Finding beauty in historical instances of ugliness is one matter but how can one find beauty in, offer one's love to, a wife who also happens to be a murderer? Angel is horrified at the thought of Tess's deed, amazed and perhaps a bit frightened by her devotion to him; and his

explanation of her behavior is the same cruelly class-conscious explanation he offered upon learning she had borne a child by Alec: an
"obscure strain in the d'Urberville blood had led to this aberration"
(372). He has reverted to judging her by her past, ancestral as well as
personal, rather than by her future; he is back to judging her "biographically" rather than "constructively." If "[t]enderness was abso-
lutely dominant in Clare at last" (373), something other than
tenderness prompts his reply when she asks him, "[D]o you think we
shall meet again after we are dead?" His response is a dodge in the
form of a kiss, "to avoid a reply at such a time" (380): "Like a greater
than himself, to the critical question at the critical time he did not
answer" (381).

Hardy's allusion here is to Matt. 26:62–63 and 27:11–12, where
Jesus, summoned by the authorities to explain to them how he can
claim to be the Son of God, refuses to answer. Hardy's analogy—
between Angel Clare refusing sympathy to Tess and the Son of God
refusing to explain himself—invites speculation. Given Angel's knowledge of Tess's simple faith, her devotional love for him, and her utter
desperation, his silence is her spiritual execution, strong evidence that
her claims on his tenderness, the last claims she possesses, are not
complete; nor will they ever be. If Angel believes that Tess is mad, why
can he not treat her question as madness and humor her in it? Angel
has serious intellectual reasons for doubting the idea of life after death,
but if tenderness toward Tess reigns in him at last, why should intellectual questions be present in his mind at this moment? Despite his
wish to judge Tess by her intentions rather than by her deeds, and in
doing so, to see beauty in her moral failures, Angel remains silent and
aloof from, blind to, her womanly purity, her ugly beauty, her very
humanity. Angel's intelligence, governed by "a hard logical deposit,
like a vein of metal in a soft loam, which turned the edge of everything
that attempted to traverse it . . . blocked his acceptance of Tess" (237).

Hardy unravels the poetry of Tess's anguish, the strange and unorthodox beauty with which he endows her impassioned suffering, in
depicting her in the final phase through Angel's thought. At the same
time that he drives his story of her pure womanliness toward revela-

tion of beauty in ugliness, he moves his central male character, the character whose grasp of Tess's beauty in ugliness is critical to the story, toward asserting the opposite: that beauty dwells only in purity, goodness, and truth, which are forever estranged from impurity, evil, and falseness.

Contrasting the beaugly and Angel's worldview creates an opposition one contemplates but does not resolve. On the one hand, one sees in the beaugliness of the major episodes a redemptive possibility, an escape from suffering through the discovery of beauty in repugnance; on the other hand, one sees, from the point of view of Angel Clare, no release from suffering because of the immutability of things. For Angel, Tess was, and will always be, one person that suddenly became another, lesser person; for him, there is no correcting this grotesque sleight of hand (226). For him, finally, except as sources of pathos and moral admonition, ugliness, defect, and impurity have no value, no beaugliness, just as there is no life after death, no meaning beyond recorded history, because ideas of "things beyond" or "life after" are irrational and not founded in experience. Hardy's use of Angel to urge that there is *no* beauty in the uglinesses of Tess's career should be taken seriously as Hardy's attempt to question his concept of beaugliness, to doubt the doubting of traditional values implicit in the concept of the beaugly.

Although Hardy achieves in Tess a great portrait of tragic humanity, in Angel he offers a memorable portrait of equal importance if less emotional appeal, the embodiment of doubting, drifting humanity incapable of unconditional love because incapable of radical belief in human worth. In light of the cry for fair treatment that Hardy sounds throughout the novel, it would be incautious to dismiss Angel Clare as merely a fool, a mule, a prig, or a snob. If one sets aside for the moment Angel's devotion to sexual purity and considers the daring of his attempt to live outside the sphere his family desires for him, he is a deeply interesting, venturesome, independent-minded character. He is certainly more appealing than his self-righteous brothers Felix and Cuthbert; and one can only applaud his decision not to take up with the sickeningly sanctimonious Mercy Chant. His appetite for new ideas, his wish not to follow in the footsteps of his brothers and father by attending the university and pursuing a career in the church, his desire to honor the intrinsic worth of people apart from their class connections, his appetite for the hard work of dairy farming, his willingness to try to change his mind about Tess, and his sense of his own intellectual inadequacies—all these things make him a complex character—even if his actions are not always admirable.

The division in Angel between modern thought and traditional feeling makes him, much more than Tess, our intellectual and emotional contemporary. His attempt to strike out on his own path by turning from the religious to the farming life, by substituting manual labor for study, by cultivating ideas uncongenial to those of his parents, and by marrying beneath his class places him nearer the concerns of many thoughtful readers of the 1990s than do Tess's exquisite agonizings over her loss of innocence. In a real sense, there is more to Angel Clare than Tess herself sees, for all her devotion to him. Tess cannot fathom how her confession to him on the wedding night stuns this man who is launched on a social and intellectual adventure filled with enough danger to his sense of identity to make him specially vulnerable to discovering a moral defect in the person he loves, the person with whom he hopes to anchor his wayward living.

For those for whom beauty does not, or cannot, dwell with ugliness, and in the novel Angel is preeminent among them, the price is removal from those things of the world conventional thought decrees undesirable, unbecoming, distasteful. Gandhi observed that to be aloof from the unbeauties, the many and varied untouchables of the world, is to be aloof from a great deal indeed. This removal is both a curse and a blessing: a curse because it curtails perception and experience; a blessing because removal is a door to what some call morality, to a good and responsible life, to a way to live and prosper amidst the imperfections of the world. An ancient Italian saying warns that "to lie down with dogs is to wake up with fleas," and Angel Clare is acquiescing before the harsh wisdom of this maxim when he sees "that he had utterly wrecked his career by this marriage," and though "on his own account he cared very little about his career . . . he had wished to make it at least a respectable one on account of his parents and brothers" (258). No doubt Clare has occasion to recall this regret when he learns, upon his return from Brazil, that his beautiful wife, now the daughter-in-law in a respectable clerical family, is not just an adulterer but a murderer as well.

Finally, then, Clare is important because in him Hardy exhibits a struggle to hold to family and to wife, to social convention *and* to social experiment, to morality *and* to something beyond morality. There can be no doubt that more difficulty lies before him, for Angel, as he departs Wintoncester and leaves behind the body of his executed wife, holding Tess's sister's hand in his, is no more certain than before of his destination. Will he marry his deceased wife's sister? Will he continue the farming life? Will he leave England for foreign parts? Will he find a way to reconcile himself to his family? Will he ever recover his temporary awareness of beauty in ugliness, beauty in defect, beauty in deficiency? Will he ever come to think and feel beyond the limits of logic and empirical reasoning?

•   •   •

I have found it a fruitful critical exercise when trying to decide what to make of Angel to invite a brief speculative account of his future. Few students respond with a sketch of a happy life with Liza-Lu. Few project reconciliation with his family. The majority imagine him continuing as a genteel English farmer of sorts, with Liza-Lu at his side. Several students claim to discover in Angel an enormous capacity, even an appetite, for unhappiness—rooted in his failure to find a substitute for the religious faith, family values, and class assumptions he has jettisoned. As one student put it, "Clare junked some pretty valuable things without having anything better, or even equally good."

Perhaps the most memorable of such accounts predicts Clare will marry Liza-Lu, find her for a time the embodiment of the beauty in purity her sister Tess was not, then, wholly consistent with his behavior in previous relationships, find her wanting. The abandonment of his family, the abandonment of Tess on the wedding night and again after her execution, the abandonment of Izz, according to this account, will in Angel's marriage to Liza-Lu become abandonment within marriage, an emotional abandonment that will enable Angel to savor domestic pleasures and at the same time indulge his deep need to punish those nearest him who do not fulfill his idealized ambitions for them. This will include his children, of whom the writer declares there will be many, and of whom Angel will have impossible expectations, and whom he will desert emotionally, financially, psychologically, retreating further and further into his world of unrealized ideals. But Angel Clare will never, never, this writer declares, recover a glimmer of the beaugly; nay, he will be unable to recall that he ever contemplated such a thing. Angel will die by the hand of Liza-Lu, who, drawing on the folk wisdom of her mother, will poison his food because she will have come to know him for the dangerously abusive man he is: one who at any cost will have persons around him conform to his impossible idealism. Liza-Lu will go unpunished, for she will have poisoned him so cunningly that it will be thought that Clare died of a weak heart; and that, declares this completer of Hardy's *Tess*, "is entirely as it should be, for Angel Clare's heart was never strong."

A more discerning view, not altogether complete, is present in a bit of dialogue written by another student of *Tess*. Angel and Liza-Lu have married, there have been no children, and well along in years, they are talking of the past:

[Liza-Lu:] 'I have been thinking of Tess, Angel.'

[Angel:] 'Ay, she's never far from my mind.'

[Liza-Lu:] 'After all these years, can we not now visit her grave?'

[Angel:] 'It is forty miles there and back, and there will be the cost of the inn, and the rains have made bogs of the roads. And who will I find to manage while we're gone?'

[Liza-Lu:] 'She is my sister.'

[Angel:] 'She was my wife, . . . but circumstances contrived to prevent her remaining my wife, . . . she could not be what she wished to be to me, and I could not help her.'

NOTES AND REFERENCES

1. Although Hardy cites Psalm 141 in his epigraph to this poem, the passage he quotes appears in Psalm 142 and differs slightly. *The Complete Poems of Thomas Hardy*, ed. James Gibson (London: Macmillan, 1976), 168; cited hereafter as *Complete Poems*.

2. *The Dynasts, An Epic Drama* [1903–1908], ed. Harold Orel (London: Macmillan, 1978).

3. See *Thomas Hardy: The Critical Heritage*, ed. R. G. Cox (London: Routledge & Kegan Paul, 1970), 220. For the inflammatory Bishop, see Thomas Hardy, *The Life and Work of Thomas Hardy*, ed. Michael Millgate (Athens, Ga.: University of Georgia Press, 1985), 294.

4. See Nina Auerbach, "The Rise of the Fallen Woman," *Nineteenth Century Fiction* 35 (1980), 29–52.

5. Florence Emily Hardy, *The Life of Thomas Hardy* (London: Macmillan, 1962), 213; cited hereafter as *Life*.

6. *The Letters of Henry James*, 2 vols., ed. Percy Lubbock (New York: Scribner's, 1920), vol. 1, 190; for the phrase from Leavis, see *The Great Tradition: George Eliot, Henry James, Joseph Conrad* [1948] (New York: New York University Press, 1967), 23.

7. "On *Tess of the d'Urbervilles*," in her *The English Novel: Form and Function* (New York: Harper & Row, 1953), 238, 241.

8. In *Modern Critical Interpretations*, ed. Harold Bloom (New York: Celsea House, 1987), 9.

9. In *Modern Critical Interpretations*, ed. Harold Bloom (New York: Chelsea House, 1987), 61–86.

10. *Collected Letters of Thomas Hardy*, 7 vols., ed. R. L. Purdy and M. Millgate (Oxford: Clarendon Press, 1978–1990), vol. 1, 250.

11. "The Profitable Reading of Fiction" (1888), in *Thomas Hardy's Personal Writings*, ed. Harold Orel (Lawrence: University of Kansas Press, 1966), 112; cited hereafter as *Personal Writings*.

Notes and References

12. "The Novels of Thomas Hardy" 1928), in *The Common Reader,* Second Series (London: Hogarth Press, 1932), 248.

13. *Return of the Native,* New Wessex Edition (London: Macmillan, 1974), 34; cited hereafter as *Return.*

14. *Tess of the d'Urbervilles,* World's Classics Edition, ed. Juliet Grindle and Simon Gatrell (Oxford & New York: Oxford University Press, 1988), 81–82; page numbers cited hereafter in the text.

15. *The Collected Poems of William Butler Yeats* (London: Macmillan, 1967), 202–205.

16. Edmund Burke, *A Philosophical Enquiry into the Origin of Our Ideas of the Sublime and the Beautiful* [1757], ed. J. T. Boulton (London: Routledge & Paul; New York: Columbia University Press, 1958), 39; cited hereafter as Burke.

17. As Hardy remarked in *The Life of Thomas Hardy,* "What has been written cannot be blotted. Each new style of novel must be the old with added ideas, not an ignoring and avoiding of the old. And so of religion, and a good many other things" (218).

18. For more on Hardy's revisions of *Tess,* see John Tudor Laird, *The Shaping of Tess of the d'Urbervilles* (Oxford: Clarendon Press, 1975; also John Tudor Laird, "New Light on the Evolution of *Tess of the d'Urbervilles,*" *Review of English* Studies 31 (1980): 414–35.

SELECTED BIBLIOGRAPHY

Primary Sources

Thomas Hardy first published *Tess of the d'Urbervilles* in 24 weekly install-ments (4 July to 26 December 1891) in the *Graphic*. He published elsewhere the episodes in which he describes Alec's violation of Tess (chapters 10–11) and Tess's baptism of her dying child (chapter 14) because the *Graphic*'s editor found them objectionable on the grounds of bad taste. The manuscript of *Tess* is in the British Museum.

The critical edition of *Tess* edited by Juliet Grindle and Simon Gatrell is very helpful in revealing Hardy's revisions (Oxford: Clarendon Press, 1983). This edition, with notes and introductory material abbreviated, is available in pa-perback in Oxford's World's Classics (Oxford & New York, 1983). Simon Gatrell has also edited a facsimile of the manuscript of *Tess* (New York: Gar-land, 1986).

Another useful paperback *Tess* is the Norton Critical Edition (3d Edition), edited by Scott Elledge (New York: W. W. Norton & Co., 1990). Elledge's *Tess* includes background materials and criticism.

The standard edition of Hardy's letters is *The Collected Letters of Thomas Hardy*, 7 vols., ed. Richard L. Purdy and Michael Millgate (Oxford University Press, 1978–1990).

Between 1888 and 1891, at the time Hardy was writing *Tess*, he published three essays on fiction that provide a helpful context for study of the novel: "The Profitable Reading of Fiction" (1888), "Candour in English Fiction" (1890), and "The Science of Fiction" (1891). These essays are available in *Thomas Hardy's Personal Writings*, ed. Harold Orel (Lawrence: The Univer-sity of Kansas Press, 1966).

Lennart Björk has edited Hardy's literary notebooks (London & Basingstoke: Macmillan, 1985). Richard Taylor has edited Hardy's personal notebooks (London & Basingstoke: Macmillan, 1978).

Selected Bibliography

Secondary Sources

Contemporary Reviews of Tess

The following reviews, which call attention to the striking originality of *Tess*, are collected, with others, in *Thomas Hardy: The Critical Heritage*, ed. Reginald C. Cox (London: Routledge & Kegan Paul, 1970), 178–248.

Anonymous. *Saturday Review* (January 1892). "Mr. Hardy . . . tells an unpleasant story in a very unpleasant way."

Black, Clementina. *Illustrated London News* (January 1892). *Tess* is "An open challenge" to that "traditional pattern of right and wrong which it is the essence of conventionality to regard as immutable."

Hutton, Richard Holt. *Spectator* (January 1892). "A story which, in spite of its almost unrivalled power, . . . is very difficult to read, because in almost every page the mind rebels against . . . the untrue picture of a universe so blank and godless."

Hannigan, Denis F. *Westminster Review* (December 1892). "The author of *Tess* . . . has revolutionized English fiction."

Lang, Andrew. *Longman's Magazine* (November 1892). "[This story is] forbidding in conception . . . because [it is] a story with a moral, . . . that moral being . . . the malignant topsy-turviness of things."

Morris, Mowbray. *Quarterly Review* (April 1892). "A queer story, [an] extremely disagreeable story [told] in an extremely disagreeable manner."

Oliphant, Margaret. *Blackwood's Magazine* (March 1892). "A new creed must treat [the old story of the ruined maid] in a new way."

Watson, William. *Academy* (February 1892). "Powerful and strange in design, splendid and terrible in execution."

Biographies

Hardy, Florence Emily. *The Early Life of Thomas Hardy* and *The Later Years of Thomas Hardy*. London: Macmillan, 1929 and 1933. Published in one volume as *The Life of Thomas Hardy* (London: Macmillan, 1964); republished under the same title in a fully edited version by Michael Millgate (Athens: University of Georgia Press, 1985). Though published under Florence Hardy's name, *Life* is Hardy's autobiography in the guise of Florence Hardy's biography of him, a self-portrait Hardy wrote in the third person with the assistance of Florence.

Millgate, Michael. *Thomas Hardy: A Biography* (Oxford: Clarendon Press, 1982). To date, the most satisfactory account of Hardy's life.

Purdy, Richard L. *Thomas Hardy: A Bibliographical Study* (Oxford: Claren-

Selected Bibliography

don Press, 1954; revised 1968). Reliable account of Hardy's composition and publication of his novels and poems, and of great biographical interest.

Selected Criticism of *Tess of the d'Urbervilles*

Auerbach, Nina. "The Rise of the Fallen Woman." *Nineteenth Century Fiction* 35 (1980): 29–52. Describes attitudes toward the fallen woman in nineteenth-century British art and literature.

Childers, Mary. "Thomas Hardy: The Man Who 'Liked' Women." *Criticism* 23 (1982): 317–34. Points to contradictions in Hardy's view of the situation of women.

Bonica, Charlotte. "Nature and Paganism in Hardy's *Tess of the d'Urbervilles*." *Journal of English Literary History* 49 (1982): 849–62. Studies Hardy's inclination to depict Nature in aesthetic rather than moral terms.

Boumelha, Penny. "*Tess of the d'Urbervilles*." In *Thomas Hardy and Women: Sexual Ideology and Narrative Form*. Sussex: The Harvester Press, 1982, 117–34. Explores Hardy's urge toward narrative androgyny.

Brady, Kristin. "Tess and Alec: Rape or Seduction?" *Thomas Hardy Annual* 4, ed. Norman Page. London: Macmillan, 1986, 127–47. Details Hardy's changes in his conception of Tess.

Casagrande, Peter. *Hardy's Influence on the Modern Novel*. London: Macmillan, 1987. Reveals *Tess* to be the novel by Hardy most influential on later novelists. See especially 204–16.

Childers, Mary. "Thomas Hardy: The Man Who 'Liked' Women." *Criticism* 23 (1982): 317–34.

Furbank, P. N. Introduction to *Tess of the d'Urbervilles*, new Wessex Edition. London: Macmillan, 1974, 11–26. Covers Hardy's representation of life aesthetically, as an amoral spectacle.

Guerard, Albert J. *Thomas Hardy* [1949]. New York: New Directions, 1964. Studies Hardy's departures from traditional realism, psychology, and plotting.

Jacobus, Mary. "Tess: The Making of a Pure Woman," in *Tearing the Veil: Essays on Femininity*, ed. Susan Lipshitz. Boston: Routledge & Kegan Paul, 1978, 77–92. Views Tess's purity as a literary fabrication designed to meet objections of reviewers.

Kramer, Dale. *Thomas Hardy: The Forms of Tragedy*. Detroit: Wayne State University Press, 1975, 111–36. Explores the aesthetic effect of *Tess* based on the principle that perception shapes both the meaning and importance of experience.

Laird, John Tudor. *The Shaping of Tess of the d'Urbervilles*. Oxford: Clarendon Press, 1975. Traces the writing of *Tess* from Hardy's earliest efforts to the 1920 reprint of the Wessex Edition of 1912.

———. "New Light on the Evolution of *Tess of the d'Urbervilles*." *Review of English Studies* 31 (1980): 414–35. Supplements *The Shaping of Tess*.

Leavis, F. R. *The Great Tradition: George Eliot, Henry James, Joseph Conrad* [1948]. London: Chatts & Windus, 1967.

Lecercle, Jean Jacques. "The Violence of Style in *Tess of the d'Urbervilles*," in *Alternative Hardy*, ed. Lance St. John Butler. London: Macmillan, 1989, 1–25. Studies Tess as both the subject and the object of violence that is primarily linguistic.

Miller, J. Hillis. "*Tess of the d'Urbervilles*: Repetition as Immanent Design," in *Thomas Hardy's Tess of the d'Urbervilles: Modern Critical Interpretations*, ed. Harold Bloom. New York: Chelsea House, 1987, 61–86. Points to the importance of repetition in *Tess*, with special reference to chapter 11.

Morgan, Rosemarie. *Women and Sexuality in the Novels of Thomas Hardy*. London and New York: Routledge, 1988, 84–109. Disputes the notion that Tess is a passive victim.

Paris, Bernard J. "'A Confusion of Many Standards': Conflicting Value Systems in *Tess of the d'Urbervilles*." *Nineteenth Century Fiction* 24 (1969): 57–92. Studies the thematic incoherence of *Tess*.

Poole, Adrian. "'Men's Words' and Hardy's Women." *Essays in Criticism* 31 (1981): 328–45. Investigates Hardy's awareness of the way men's language delimits women.

Silverman, Kaja. "History, Figuration, and Female Subjectivity in *Tess of the d'Urbervilles*." *Novel* 18 (1984): 5–28. Inspects Hardy's narrative technique in *Tess*.

Tanner, Tony. "Colour and Movement in Hardy's *Tess of the d'Urbervilles*," in *Modern Critical Interpretations*, ed. Harold Bloom, 9–23. Examines the imagery in *Tess*.

Van Ghent, Dorothy. "On *Tess of the d'Urbervilles*," in *The English Novel: Form and Function*. New York: Harper & Row, 1953, 236–55. Analyzes the style in *Tess*.

Wickens, G. Glen. "Hardy and the Aesthetic Mythographers: The Myth of Demeter and Persephone in *Tess of the d'Urbervilles*." *University of Toronto Quarterly* 53 (1984): 85–106. Surveys Hardy's use of myth in *Tess* and suggests the question of Tess's purity is partly an aesthetic one.

Woolf, Virginia. "The Novels of Thomas Hardy," in *The Common Reader*, Second Series. London: Hogarth Press, 1932, 245–57. An incisive account of Hardy's strengths and weaknesses as a novelist.

INDEX

Index

Index

THE AUTHOR

Peter J. Casagrande is professor of English and associate dean of Arts and Sciences at the University of Kansas in Lawrence. He is the author of *Unity in Hardy's Novels: "Repetitive Symmetries"* (1982) and *Hardy's Influence on the Modern Novel* (1987) and is currently at work on a study of Hardy's originality.